GET IT
DONE!

101 WAYS TO THINK AND ACT SMART

"In any moment of decision the best thing you can do is the right thing, the next best thing is the wrong thing, and the worst thing you can do is nothing."

Theodore Roosevelt (1858–1919)

GET IT DONE!

101 WAYS TO THINK AND ACT SMART

DARREN BRIDGER & DAVID LEWIS

DUNCAN BAIRD PUBLISHERS

LONDON

GET IT DONE!

Darren Bridger & David Lewis

Distributed in the USA and Canada by Sterling Publishing Co., Inc.
387 Park Avenue South, New York, NY 10016-8810

This edition first published in the UK and USA in 2008 by
Duncan Baird Publishers Ltd
Sixth Floor, Castle House, 75–76 Wells Street, London W1T 3QH

Managing Editor: Caroline Ball
Editor: Katie John
Assistant Editor: Kirty Topiwala
Managing Designer: Clare Thorpe
Commissioned illustrations: Bonnie Dain for Lilla Rogers Studio

Library of Congress Cataloging-in-Publication Data Available
ISBN-13: 978-1-84483-586-7   ISBN-10: 1-84483-586-3

10 9 8 7 6 5 4 3 2 1

Typeset in Trade Gothic
Color reproduction by Scanhouse, Malaysia
Printed and bound in China

For information about custom editions, special sales, premium and corporate
purchases, please contact Sterling Special Sales Department at 800-805-5489
or specialsales@sterlingpub.com.

CONTENTS

INTRODUCTION

Every day we analyze situations, tackle problems, make choices, take decisions, act upon them. This book shows you how to do all of these things better. We'll explain how to use techniques developed by psychologists, mathematicians, business consultants, sports competitors and even military strategists. There are mind-training exercises and self-assessments, as well as background information to inform and entertain. All of these tools can help you to use your mental powers more effectively.

FACING CHALLENGES

Occasionally, a situation will demand an instant response – if we see a poisonous snake in our path, we don't spend a lot of time weighing up options! But most situations are much more complex than this, and demand a variety of reasoning skills. Even an everyday decision such as choosing a vacation can involve a surprisingly complex process: estimating risks, weighing up options, considering the needs of others, and predicting how we might feel in different locations.

Sometimes, an area of life – work, family life or even leisure time – can give rise to problems that can be difficult to tackle or solve. You might find that you can't manage a situation effectively with your usual strategies, or even that it presents you with an entirely new dilemma. In these circumstances, you might well need extra mental tools. This book will guide you through every stage of a challenge, so that you can work your way to an appropriate conclusion.

FOCUSING YOUR MIND

As a starting point, you'll need a variety of mental skills to help you analyze the situation. First, you need to be able to focus – to use your mind like a camera to obtain the best view of the problem. There are times when your focus will have to be pin-sharp, but at other times you may need to take a wide-angle view, or to adjust your thinking so that you look deeper into the background of an issue. The first two chapters show you different ways in which you can draw on both logical reasoning and more creative, intuitive thought, so that you'll be able to cope successfully with a wide range of situations.

DECISIONS, DECISIONS

Every choice brings unique opportunities, but also costs: for every option that you take, there will be one or more others that you have to reject. The worry about making the right choice, or the suspicion that a discarded option might actually have been better, can make decision-making fraught with anxiety and lead to regret.

You can do one of two things when decision-making: exhaustively consider every possible choice in the quest for the perfect answer, or search just until you find a good enough option. In confining yourself to looking for the perfect answer, there's a risk that you might expend a disproportionate amount of time and energy, and perhaps still not attain your ideal, when all you need is simply a workable solution.

The more elements there are for you to weigh up in your mind, the more skillful you'll need to be to narrow down your options to a precise course of action. You may have to take into account all kinds of conditional factors – you'll do X if this happens and Y if that happens – but without a clear set of steps that can lead you to a decision, it's easy to become entangled in a web of confusion. Making these choices may at times seem like hard work, but the alternative is worse: as the philosopher Bertrand Russell wrote, "Nothing is so exhausting as indecision. And nothing is so futile."

THINKING STRAIGHT

Effective decision-making doesn't always come naturally. However, it can be learnt and improved. To start with, you need a clear perception of the facts: if you fail to check your assumptions, then no matter how good your reasoning, you could be misguided. You're equipped with a range of inbuilt reflexes, emotional responses and reasoning skills, which are often useful but can sometimes lead to errors of thinking. By learning how to recognize and avoid these biases, you can keep your mind clear and your perceptions accurate.

Recognizing when there's one route to success and when there are many, even knowing when *not* to decide, are all part of the decision-making process, as is a judicious assessment of the risks. And, as with any type of mental process, it's important not to let stress or anxiety sabotage your thinking – a vital point on which Chapter 5 offers a wealth of practical guidance.

A samurai was traditionally supposed to be able to arrive at any decision within the space of seven breaths. While you might not achieve or even need such clarity, with the help of this book you can discover the benefits of sharper, more assured decision-making.

TIME FOR ACTION

Some people spend an inordinate time analyzing situations without ever making concrete decisions; others make good decisions but then fail to act on them. Procrastination, flagging motivation and "waiting for the right moment" can all prevent us from taking action. So can fear: fear of the consequences (many reasonable and valid actions have a downside), fear of change, or fear of others' reactions.

To overcome these obstacles and turn your decisions into effective action, you'll need to define a clear goal, have a well-crafted plan of action, manage your time efficiently, and break out of inertia to create a new "habit" of action. By mastering these necessary skills, you'll be able to achieve your objectives as easily and effectively as possible.

STRETCH YOURSELF

Whether you wish to work through the whole book or simply dip into sections that interest you, we hope that you'll find this a fascinating, enlightening and instructive practical guide to the most valuable tool you have at your disposal – your own mind. Your resources and your potential capabilities go far beyond what you might imagine. Learn to stretch yourself a little: you'll never regret it!

"Do you want to know who you are? Don't ask. Act!"

Thomas Jefferson (1743–1826)

CHAPTER 1

FOCUS AND CONCENTRATION

To tackle any decision or take any action, it's essential for you to be able to focus your thinking effectively. However, narrow, single-minded concentration isn't the best option in every situation. This chapter shows you how you can benefit from changing mental "gear" to respond to different circumstances. There are exercises to help you discover your preferred style of thinking, and to teach you how best to use both analytical and creative thinking to get results. Lastly, there are guidelines on multi-tasking and on setting priorities for your activities.

FOCUSING EFFECTIVELY

Problem-solving, decision-making and action all need to start with the right level of focus. To tackle all the possible aspects of a project or plan, you'll need to be able to switch between different types of focus, from constructive daydreaming to intense concentration.

THE FOUR LEVELS OF FOCUS

The mind has four main levels of focus, a bit like the gears of a car. These levels result from different patterns of brain activity, which are described opposite. You naturally make use of all four, but it's also possible for you to "change gear" consciously.

Changing down

To drop down to gears 2 or 1, find somewhere you won't be disturbed, close your eyes lightly and relax. Keep your breathing slow and deep, at four breaths per minute for 60 seconds. The most helpful situations include taking a bath or shower, walking, or sitting or lying down. Slow, soothing music will help you change right down to first gear.

Changing up

To move up to gears 3 or 4, sit upright and breathe slightly faster — say 16 to 24 breaths per minute — for one minute. Small amounts of caffeine (such as coffee or cola) can give you a quick boost. However, beware that your focus doesn't go into overdrive and become anxiety.

THE MIND'S GEARS

During the last century, scientists researching the brain identified four main electrical frequency bands which we use in thinking. As we think, large clusters of brain cells emit rhythmic electrical pulses. The faster the rhythms, the more concentrated the thinking. These frequency bands can be seen as the "gears" of the mind.

* * * * *

Gear 1: slow activity (theta brain state). Occurs during sleeping and daydreaming; focus is almost completely inward.

* * *

Gear 2: medium activity (alpha brain state). Relaxed alertness, mainly focused inward, but prepared for action.

* * *

Gear 3: fast activity (beta brain state). Concentration and intellectual challenge.

* * *

Gear 4: very fast activity (high beta brain state). Intense concentration, which can easily turn into anxiety.

* * *

Gears 1 and 2 are great for creative thinking and for tapping into your intuition because they enable you to reach into your subconscious and combine ideas from different brain regions. Gears 3 and 4 are the best choices for logical thinking and for close attention to specific issues.

MAINTAINING CONCENTRATION

Later on in the book, we'll see how "directed daydreaming" can help you in making choices, but when you're actually analyzing or solving a specific problem, you have to be able to concentrate. To help you maintain your mental focus, there are three principal aspects that you'll need to control.

DECISIVENESS

You need to know when to make an instant decision and when it's better to take your time – like choosing a fast or slow shutter speed on a camera. If you're feeling swamped with choices, try not to jump blindly into action, or to procrastinate. Look at the section "Focusing on solutions" (see page 45) to find a way through the confusion. Ask yourself whether it would be right to decide or act now, or better to wait and take into account all the possibilities. If you're ready for an instant solution, turn your mind up to fourth gear ... and go for it.

PERSISTENCE

Not all problem-solving can take place instantly. For some challenges, you'll need time to come up with a solution, and will have to maintain a longer-term focus on them. Set aside time each hour, day or week, as appropriate, for a blast of high focus on your issue. Try not to go over and over old ground: each "blast" should result in a move forward. Between "blasts", your subconscious mind will be working away on the issue, noting any new information that could be pertinent.

PURPOSE

To maintain a high level of concentration, especially for complex tasks, you need to eliminate distractions from your surroundings so you can keep your mind on what you're supposed to be doing.

The smallest things can disrupt your thoughts. A song on the radio, for instance, might go around and around in your head, triggering random ideas and memories, which might then arouse emotions, which might give rise to further thoughts, and so on.

Learn to notice when your thoughts are drifting, particularly if they go in a negative direction. As soon as this happens, tell yourself STOP and bring your focus back to the task at hand. This technique works because it's impossible to hold two ideas in your mind simultaneously: the word STOP disrupts the distracting train of thought. For a stronger effect, you could try wearing a rubber band around your wrist, and snapping it gently on your skin whenever you think STOP. Don't worry if you don't achieve perfect results straight away – it may take repeated attempts. But you'll become better at it over time.

MAP YOUR DAILY RHYTHMS

Most of us concentrate best at particular times of the day. If you don't already know which time is best for you, try this exercise. In a notebook, make a daily record of your concentration at specific times of day. Rate each time from 1 (not able to focus at all) to 7 (perfect). Record each day on a separate page, so that you're not influenced by your previous ratings. When you've done this for at least a week, look back through all your ratings and see which times of day were best for you.

YOUR FOCUS STYLE

Confronted by an unfamiliar challenge or problem, most people tend to focus on the information available in one of two distinctly different ways, each of which has advantages and drawbacks. Discover your preferred style by answering A or B to each of the statements given below.

DISCOVER YOUR FOCUS STYLE

1 When choosing a new electrical item, I principally base my decision on:
   A product reviews and careful comparison of features
   B which one I feel most drawn to by its look or feel.

2 When deciding on a vacation destination, I usually:
   A conduct in-depth research and take my time
   B choose on the basis of what catches my eye.

3 When deciding on a course of action, I:
   A plan the steps that lead to my carefully specified goal
   B know roughly what my goal is but work out how best to get there as I go.

4 I feel happiest when I know:
   A the single best way of achieving a particular goal
   B the full range of options open to me.

5   When working toward a solution to a complex problem, I:
    A   proceed one step at a time
    B   keep my eyes on the big picture.

6   I firmly believe that what matters most in life is:
    A   achieving clearly defined goals
    B   exploring the full range of possibilities.

7   When working toward a goal, I prefer to:
    A   follow a detailed plan
    B   think on my feet as I go along.

8   I would sooner learn how to do something by:
    A   studying it in depth and mastering the rules
    B   finding out by trial and error.

9   If I lose something at home, I start by:
    A   methodically searching all the places where it could be
    B   having a quick look around the most likely places.

10 When solving a problem, I spend more time on:
    A   studying all the details
    B   coming up with as many different solutions as possible.

Count up your A responses and then your B responses, and see on the next page how to interpret your conclusions.

WHAT YOUR FOCUS STYLE MEANS

If you had more As than Bs, then your natural focus style is that of a Pathfinder. More Bs than As means that your focus style is that of a Pilot. An equal or nearly equal number of As and Bs indicates that you can switch style according to the problem or decision. The ideal is to be proficient in both styles of focus, since this promotes flexible, creative, highly adaptive thinking.

PATHFINDERS

Pathfinders adopt a methodical, step-by-step approach to gathering information, and are detail-oriented. This style works best when there could be factors that need to be uncovered, and when you have plenty of time. It's most effective for technical problems and for "convergent problems" (see page 40), which have single or few solutions.

The main drawback of this style is that it leads you to expect just one solution, whereas there might be multiple possibilities.

Use the Pathfinder style by:

- collecting as many facts as possible
- studying how other people have solved similar problems
- writing down all of your possible options and listing their pros and cons (see Chapter 4)
- plotting every step toward your goal.

PILOTS

Pilots prefer to take a broader, high-level view of information. They tend to rely on intuition, gut feelings and hunches (often based on previous experience) as they seek many possible solutions. The Pilot style works best with "divergent problems" (see page 40), which have several equally viable answers. It offers original, creative solutions. It's also ideal if time is short, or for situations in which rules can change or new options arise rapidly.

The drawback of the Pilot style is that in cases where there are just one or a few solutions, but the way to reach them isn't obvious, this approach won't help you to identify the steps you need to take.

Use the Pilot style by:

- considering the "big picture" and gaining a broad overview of possible solutions
- using creative techniques (see Chapter 2) to generate a list of as many solutions as possible
- starting off by making any move which takes you closer to your goal, and then reconsidering your options
- trusting yourself and recognizing that your gut feelings about a choice can often give rise to the best decision.

There are tips in Chapters 3 and 4 on improving Pathfinder skills, and Chapter 2 includes guidance on improving Pilot skills.

WHEN AND HOW TO MULTI-TASK

Busy lifestyles often require us to perform several different tasks at once. Multi-tasking is a useful skill, but we also need to learn to recognize when attempting too many things is likely to disrupt our focus and prevent us from carrying out jobs quickly or effectively.

CONFLICTING DEMANDS ON THE MIND

Doing several tasks at once presents few difficulties when these activities are routine, but in more important and mentally demanding challenges – such as making a life-changing decision, writing reports at work, or helping a child with homework – multi-tasking can prove counter-productive. Attempting to do too many things simultaneously, or even in rapid succession, results in poor levels of attention, loss of concentration, impaired memory and, frequently, error-prone thinking.

The main reason for these failures lies in the fact that multi-tasking divides the brain's processing power between the different activities, significantly reducing its ability to work efficiently, especially when tasks make very similar demands.

Different parts of the brain specialize in different activities, such as listening, looking, movement and language. Multi-tasking is hardest, and can cause most problems, whenever two or more separate tasks require the same mode of thought and so involve the same brain regions. Examples include trying to attend to two different conversations at once (conflicting listening tasks), conducting a phone conversation while reading (conflicting language tasks) or that old party favourite of attempting to rub your stomach and pat your head at the same time (conflicting movement tasks).

EFFECTIVE MULTI-TASKING

The following practical tips will help you to cope with two or more activities at the same time and still maintain the quality of your thinking in each task.

- Don't mix tasks needing the same skills (such as dialling on a cell phone while driving: both "movement" tasks). Mixing tasks that use different skills is less of a problem (such as listening to music while driving: a listening task plus a movement task).
- If you like listening to music when reading or writing, try playing only instrumental pieces, with no lyrics to make demands on your language-processing centres. Or tune in to a foreign radio station on which the lyrics and speech might be less distracting.
- When you need to switch from one important task to another, take a break between them to refresh your mind. Alternatively, intersperse complex mental tasks with undemanding routine activities, such as taking a walk or washing up.

STOP!
You must always avoid mixing tasks that might conflict:
- when you need your performance to be the best it can be, such as when preparing an important piece of work
- when it's critical to avoid making mistakes, such as when driving.

SETTING PRIORITIES

To get things done, we need to focus our mental and physical energies effectively. The best way to concentrate on vital tasks and avoid distractions is to set priorities, rather than simply reacting to whatever immediately presents itself.

WORK AND FAMILY, REST AND PLAY

Before embarking on any activity, start by reminding yourself of your priorities in life. There's no point in finding very practical or creative solutions if they're out of step with your own values or beliefs.

Everything we do or seek to do falls into one of four categories:
- work (including charitable work and domestic chores)
- relationships and family
- hobbies and leisure (including education for its own pleasure)
- health (including spiritual practices, such as meditation or yoga).

Which of these areas is your current priority? Which is the overall priority in your life? How many hours do you devote to each area per week? You may be surprised to find that you're spending a lot of time on one area, yet it has nothing to do with your main goals in life.

WHAT'S TOP OF THE LIST?

All too often priorities are dictated by whatever requires the most urgent attention, such as daily work chores, paying bills and responding to requests from others. You can become overly reactive, like a person standing in front of a tennis-ball-firing machine, frantically batting away an onslaught of balls, but never having time to pause to make any other movement. While life is firing the "urgent but not important" tasks at you, the not urgent but potentially life-enriching activities remain neglected in the background.

PRIORITIZING THE LIFE-ENHANCERS

The matrix below includes four categories of task, classified according to how urgent and/or life-enhancing they are. To help establish your priorities, draw up your own task matrix. Divide a sheet of paper into quarters, and list each of your tasks under the headings shown.

TASK MATRIX	
urgent and life-enhancing	urgent but not life-enhancing
life-enhancing but not urgent	neither urgent nor life-enhancing

For each task, ask yourself the following question before adding it to the matrix: "How will carrying out this task help me to achieve any of my priorities in life?"

Keep your matrix within easy reach and tick off each task as you finish it. Of course, you can't always avoid the "urgent but not life-enhancing" tasks, but make sure that these (or, worse, the "neither urgent nor life-enhancing" jobs) aren't the only ones being ticked off. Take care to free up time for the things that are truly important to you.

CHAPTER 2

FRESH PERSPECTIVES

Taking a creative approach to an issue can help you to generate the widest possible range of choices to consider. By opening your mind and giving ideas time to grow, you may find solutions arising naturally. Brainstorming, and other forms of creative thinking, can open your mind to options you hadn't considered, or help you to see things in a new light.

You can also nourish your creative side by tapping into your subconscious mind, and by drawing on your powers of intuition. We're so used to thinking in words that we often forget we can also make use of these powerful non-verbal modes of thought. All of these imaginative techniques can provide an ideal foundation for reaching effective answers and decisions.

CULTIVATING CREATIVE SOLUTIONS

While logical thinking taps into what we think of as intelligence, creative thinking often comes from what we might classify as wisdom. When an idea or observation enters a mind rich with experience in a particular field, it flourishes and can generate exciting creative concepts.

THE FRUITS OF A FERTILE MIND

Most writers on creativity describe it as an organic, subconscious activity, in contrast to the structured, conscious form that logical decision-making takes. People often talk of someone having a "fertile imagination" or a situation being "pregnant with possibilities".

Like a seed planted in rich soil, creative ideas flourish best in a receptive, unlimiting frame of mind. You could see the process as being like the gestation of a baby. It can be divided into three stages:

- **Conception:** finding an interesting question, puzzle or problem.
- **Gestation:** letting go of trying to force an answer out and allowing the creative process to take its course.
- **Birth:** making time to relax, in order to be receptive to new ideas.

A creative approach may lead you to an original solution, but getting there can be harder work than merely choosing from a range of pre-existing options and following a logical path. In addition, it usually takes more time, as creative thinking is best done slowly. However, brainstorming is an exception; see page 30.

NURTURING
CREATIVITY

While creative thinking is not a simple step-by-step process, there are some techniques you can use to coax yourself into creative states, and increase your chances of developing ideas.

* * * * *

Be prepared. Keep notepads by your bed, in your car and to hand around the house. Good ideas don't just happen at a desk: they're actually more likely to arise while your conscious mind is on other things.

* * *

Sleep on an issue. Often, when you wake up you'll have new insights.

* * *

Keep a dream diary. We all have several dreams each night, but they soon fade from memory on waking. By keeping a dream diary you're more likely to remember them.

* * *

Exercise. Many people find they come up with their best ideas while their body is engaged in physical activity. Try walking, swimming, cycling ... or anything that keeps the body busy but allows the mind to drift freely.

* * *

Take it easy. Original ideas are most likely to emerge in times of relaxation; conversely, research shows that the more pressure people have to work under, the more rigid their thinking becomes.

BRAINSTORMING

First suggested by an advertising executive in the 1930s, brainstorming has since become a popular approach to problem-solving that is widely used in business. Although originally intended for use by groups, it's a technique that can prove even more effective when done alone.

STEP-BY-STEP BRAINSTORMING

Brainstorming involves two stages. The first is based on simply coming up with as many ideas as possible; the second is evaluation.

Set aside at least half an hour in which you can relax and will not be interrupted. Write down (or type out) 50–100 possible solutions or ideas that occur to you, no matter how crazy, off-the-wall or even unworkable. Add a star next to any that create a particularly positive emotional reaction. The requirement at this stage is quantity, not quality, of ideas – stopping to consider them will inhibit the flow and may cause you to miss a non-obvious but ultimately optimal answer.

Once you've exhausted all possible ideas, look back over your list and pay special attention to the starred items. Try rating these ideas on a scale of 1 (useless) to 7 (superb).

Finally, review all the ideas that received a 6 or 7 rating. There may be an obvious winning answer, but make sure you also look at further potential. Could any exciting but unworkable ideas be combined to create an even better solution, or could an idea be transformed by being made larger, smaller or even a different colour?

VISUAL THINKING

Many parts of the brain, including much of the right hemisphere and the subconscious, think in pictures and patterns rather than words. When faced with a problem or choice, it can often be a good idea to give these more visual parts of your mind a chance to stretch their intelligence.

DIRECTED DAYDREAMING AND VISUALIZATION

Our culture is primarily focused on expressing thoughts through language. However, we often overlook another powerful mode of thought at our disposal: our visual imagination. Generating ideas by visualization is useful not only for creative thinking, but also for managing emotions, and for goal-setting (see Chapters 5 and 6).

When you're deeply relaxed, your mind drops down to first gear (see page 15), in which it focuses inward, toward sleep and dreaming, and you begin to produce brainwaves conducive to generating mental imagery. This is the ideal state for making you receptive to creative ideas welling up from the depths of your mind.

The subconscious seems to communicate to the conscious mind by means of images. Rather than being completely random, or mere repetitions of what you've just been looking at, these mental images can be full of meaning. They can be particularly efficient at encapsulating complex, detailed ideas very quickly. You can access these images consciously: while in the daydreaming or visualizing state of mind, dive down into your subconscious and retain any that seem particularly powerful or significant. You can then think about their meaning at greater length once you've brought yourself back to a normal waking state of mind.

KICKSTARTING VISUAL IMAGERY

Visualizing is a skill like any other: the more you practise it, the easier it becomes. Letting your mind wander as you draw works well (don't worry if you think you "can't draw"), or you can generate images in your mind. Alternatively, try these techniques to start the process:

- Relax and close your eyes. As you don't actually want to fall asleep, stay sitting as upright as possible or set a timer to alert you every five minutes or so.
- Close your eyes, and gently rub your eyelids as though you were tired. This action produces phosphenes – visual patterns resulting from pressure on the retina. Ask yourself what these flashing images remind you of.
- Stare at a window, or other area of contasting light and dark, then close your eyes. This should create an after-image. Concentrate on the image and allow it to evolve into other images.
- Sit with a view of the sky, gaze at a cloud and relax. Gradually let your imagination make shapes from the cloud's outline.

RECORDING WHAT YOU SEE

Psychologist Dr Win Wenger has demonstrated that describing visualized images out loud helps to strengthen them. He recommends starting with a specific question that you wish to put to your subconscious, closing your eyes and waiting for images to appear. Then you describe – either into a tape recorder or to another person – the literal details of the images that you're receiving. Try also to include any other sensory impressions that your mind is giving you.

It's important that you don't try to analyze what you've seen until after you've finished the session, otherwise you'll introduce assumptions that could influence the images.

By keeping the recording of your session (or by making notes immediately afterwards, if you haven't recorded it) you can refer back to it later. You could save your recordings or notes and build up a record of "answers" to particular questions. You could also use this technique to record multiple sessions for the same question, building up a range of perspectives and possible solutions.

SCIENTIFIC VISIONARIES

It's not just artistic people who draw on their imagination or daydreams: some of the greatest scientists have also solved problems in this way. For example, Thomas Edison used to "sit for ideas" with a notepad in a darkened room, and it's been widely reported that Francis Crick may have been inspired by similar imaginative reveries in working out the structure of DNA. Albert Einstein performed what he called "thought experiments" – for instance, visualizing travelling on a beam of light led him toward facts that contributed to his theory of relativity. The chemist August Kekulé worked out the circular structure of benzene after dreaming of a snake with its tail in its mouth, while the engineer Nikola Tesla had the astonishing ability to visualize an invention in his imagination and know for certain whether or not it would work without ever constructing it.

TAPPING INTO YOUR INTUITION

Intuition, like creativity, is driven by the subconscious mind, and often appears impenetrable and mysterious. Unlike most types of creative thinking, intuition usually comes in "flashes", giving you instant information.

JUST A FEELING?

When first approaching a problem or decision, it's common to have an immediate, instinctive reaction. Yet you might dismiss such feelings because you don't know how you arrived at them, and can't always logically justify them. While not abandoning logic altogether, it can be very useful to pay more attention to these initial hunches, as research suggests they are more often than not correct.

Intuition is more likely to arise in an area in which you already have rich experience. For example, we are all used to interacting with people, so it's no surprise that this is an area in which we are likely to have the strongest "gut feelings" of liking or disliking, trusting or distrusting. Similarly, experts who have accumulated a lot of knowledge in a particular field are often able to make very quick and accurate subconscious evaluations by drawing on their experience.

FOLLOW YOUR INTUITION OR NOT?

Your unconscious can take in and synthesize more bits of information than your conscious mind can, so for complex choices first listen to your gut instinct, but for simple choices first attempt to reason things out. There are also two main instances when you should treat intuition with caution: first, if you're experiencing strong feelings of either fear or desire, as these could cloud your genuinely intuitive judgments; and secondly, when you're facing something about which you have little or no experience on which to base your intuition.

HOW TO MAKE THE MOST OF INTUITIVE THOUGHTS
Step 1
Look out for fleeting first impressions, as they dart across your consciousness like a butterfly. Practise capturing these feelings, using the net of your attention! Take particular note whenever you have an emotional response that seems out of proportion to the situation.

Step 2
Question your initial impression. What triggered it? What could be the reason for it? Was it some detail, picked up subconsciously, that your conscious attention failed to note as significant?

Step 3
Ask yourself the question: "What would happen if I trusted this feeling and acted on it?"

Step 4
Check your own assumptions to make sure that your response isn't based on a misconception. As we'll see on pages 76–9, reactions that "just feel right" can sometimes be based on false information.

CREATIVE RE-EVALUATION

Before diving in to solve a problem, it's worth taking time to re-evaluate it. By thinking about it differently, you may uncover a whole new perspective, which could lead to more surprising or more elegant solutions.

A SIMPLE ANSWER

We've all had the experience of seeing some new invention or solution and saying, "Why didn't I think of that?" Even solutions to complex problems are often surprisingly simple, and many of the best appear blindingly obvious once we know them. This is often the case when someone takes an idea from one area and applies it to an unrelated area — creative thinking thrives when we bring together apparently disconnected elements. For example, an engineer called Percy LeBaron Spencer invented the microwave oven after noticing that a bar of chocolate had melted in his pocket while he'd been working near a military radar system that was emitting microwave radiation.

A NEW ANGLE

Most errors in decision-making are not errors of logic, but errors of initial perception. So looking at things from different angles is an essential skill. This can be particularly useful if you typically use the Pathfinder way of thinking (see page 20). By taking a different view, you could find an answer that you might never have thought of otherwise — or you may find that the problem disappears completely.

SOME LEADING QUESTIONS

To enable you to bring fresh perspectives to bear on a problem, try some of the viewpoints suggested below.

*   *   *   *   *

Is there a problem?
How would you perceive your situation differently if you didn't see it as a problem? How would someone who saw the situation as a blessing perceive it? Try listing all the positive aspects of a negative situation.

*   *   *

Are there any useful connections?
Is there a factor connected to your issue that, taken in isolation, could lead your thoughts along a new and perhaps more productive path?

*   *   *

How would others see the situation?
How would a mathematician approach this? How about an artist? A child? Someone from the past? Someone from a different culture?

*   *   *

Are opposites really opposite?
We tend to categorize things as being the opposite of other things, but how would your perception change if you assumed that they were alike?

*   *   *

Can books help?
Libraries and bookstores have a higher concentration of ideas than anywhere else (apart from the internet). Browse through any books that catch your eye and ask yourself how they might relate to your issue.

ANALYZING OPTIONS

Analyzing your options is key to making a good decision. For example, if you're facing a problem, it's important to understand what sort of problem it is, whether or not it's actually within your control, and how it might change over time.

However, all the logic in the world, even the use of mainframe supercomputers, will be of no use if your starting assumptions are incorrect – the quality of your thinking can only be as good as the information on which your reasoning is based. While we usually believe we're reasoning through our decisions, mostly we're actually just calling on past experience to guide us, or automatically responding to cues within our immediate surroundings (without realizing it!). As Anaïs Nin said, "We don't see things as they are; we see things as we are." This chapter helps you to identify any biases in your own thinking, so your perceptions and reasoning will be clear.

CONVERGENT AND DIVERGENT PROBLEMS

A key part of making a successful decision is defining the form of problem or challenge you're facing. You need to ask yourself whether you have one particular aim or whether there could be more than one satisfactory solution. This will clarify your thinking and help with decision-making.

CONVERGENT OR DIVERGENT?

If there's only one solution to a problem, or a limited number of solutions, and an answer is either right or wrong (such as: "What is 2 + 2?"; "Which airlines fly direct to Chicago?"), the problem is classified as "convergent". If there are many possible answers and no single optimum answer (for example, what to serve at a dinner party), it's called a "divergent" problem.

It's always worth bearing in mind that more problems are divergent than convergent. Thinking that a problem is convergent when it isn't can make decision-making very much harder than it needs to be, and you can waste a tremendous amount of time, effort and worry seeking *the* solution, when what is needed is *a* solution.

The two focus styles described in Chapter 1 (see pages 20–21) come into play here. The Pathfinder style, which involves a methodical, step-by-step approach, is best for convergent problems, whereas the Pilot style, in which you take a more wide-ranging and intuitive view, is most effective for solving divergent problems.

ANALYZING OPTIONS ON A CONVERGENT PROBLEM

The trick with a convergent problem is to eliminate dead ends quickly. Imagine that two walkers, starting from the same point, are racing each other to the top of a mountain. Each adopts a different approach to the challenge.

The walker preferring a Pilot style would typically start with any move that takes him closer to the mountain. The other walker, using the Pathfinder style, would first plot his entire route by checking out the terrain on a map. In this case, he would discover that a broad river lies between them and the mountain. His companion will only discover this when he reaches the water and has to rethink his route. The Pathfinder begins with what seems a contrary move and initially walks *away* from the mountain, because he has learnt that this route leads to a path that will take him to a bridge across the river.

For a convergent problem like this, where the objective – or the solution – is limited and specific, the Pathfinder approach is the more successful. The time spent gathering all the necessary information about the route beforehand has avoided expending time and effort going down a dead end and having to go back to the starting point.

Solution trees

Since most problems don't come with a ready-made map, it's helpful to draw up your own, in the form of a solution tree, to help you find a pathway to your goal.

To construct a solution tree, you need to:

- draw a starting point (such as a box marked "START")
- draw boxes for each option, and draw lines linking them to the start
- for each option, work out a possible next step, draw a new box for it, and link the two boxes with a line
- keep adding further possible steps until you run out.

This process should highlight any dead ends and provide you with viable routes. As a simple example, the mountain problem would be laid out like this:

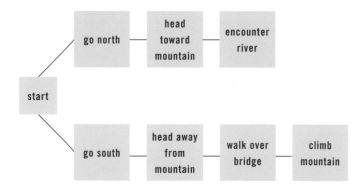

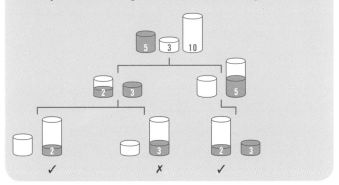

TACKLING DIVERGENT PROBLEMS

If you're dealing with an issue that could have a number of viable solutions – where to go on vacation, which TV to buy, which career to follow – the secret of success is to use the Pilot's strategy of inching your way toward a decision even when unsure of the exact path to it.

Ask questions (see pages 48–9), draw up pro and con lists (see page 66) and try creative carving (see next page) to help you take the first step. At this point, some options close and others open up. Repeat the process as you work toward an appropriate final decision.

Creative carving

This technique is an adaptation of the Pilot's strategy of making a start on a problem to see where it leads. Creative carving involves breaking down a big problem into its most obvious parts, reviewing it again, and if the solution still isn't clear, breaking those parts down into smaller elements. You continue until an answer appears.

Imagine that you're planning a family vacation. Begin with the most general solution: a few destinations that fulfil everyone's basic needs. Then ask yourself whose wishes would still have to be met. Could one of your choices be adapted to include more options? For example, if your starting point is a sightseeing vacation, are there any places near a beach, to include a few days' fun for the children? Keep going until you've accommodated as many wishes as you can.

A Venn diagram, like the one for the imaginary family below, can help you decide. Allocate a circle to each of your criteria. The best solution will fall into the central section, where all the circles meet.

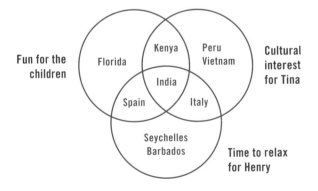

FOCUSING ON SOLUTIONS

Exhaustively going over the causes of a problem can prevent you from reaching an answer. In a form of therapy called "solution-focused brief therapy", practitioners question the need to dissect problems and suggest, instead, analyzing solutions. Here are a couple of ways in which this can work.

AS IF BY MAGIC ...
Imagine waking up tomorrow and finding that your problem has magically disappeared without warning. How would you recognize that this has happened? Go through the day in your imagination and list all the things, even the smallest ones, that would be different.

　　This technique is more than just wishful thinking. By envisaging the details of life in the future, beyond the "stalling point", you can free up your thinking and perhaps find a new perspective that helps you to minimize problems or even avoid them altogether.

ACCENTUATE THE POSITIVE
Ask yourself, "Are there times when the outcome I want already occurs?" For example, if your child wets the bed, the question to focus on is: "On which nights does my child stay dry?" If you need to earn more money, try asking, "When have I already made more money?" Or, looking at it from another angle: "When do I feel comfortable with what I earn?" If you can pinpoint any factor that you can relate to your desired outcome, however small, try to build on it.

THE LIMITS OF CONTROL

An old joke goes: "Everyone complains about the weather, but no one ever does anything about it!" While attempting to change the weather is obviously ridiculous, we often hold equally unreasonable beliefs about our ability to manage the unmanageable and control the uncontrollable.

WHERE DO YOU DRAW THE LINE?

Things we often try to control yet can't include:

- the actions of others
- the thoughts and feelings of others
- the ultimate outcome of events
- our own feelings.

We may be able to influence and manage these factors, but ultimately we can never truly master them.

Things we *can* control include:

- our own behaviour
- our own attitudes.

List the elements of your problem that are under your control and those that aren't. Focus purely on those you can control. You could even rank these elements on a scale of 1 to 7, with 1 as the easiest and 7 as the hardest, and focus on those at the bottom of the scale.

DON'T PANIC!

Many of us have felt ourselves frozen with anxiety in the face of a problem. If you ever suffer from panic like this, the following tips should help you to shake off the feeling and regain your power to act.

* * * * *

Try to avoid letting your thoughts run away with you — for example, "If I mess up this project, I'll lose my job, then I won't be able to pay my rent, then I'll lose my home …". Use the STOP technique (see page 17) to nip the panic in the bud.

* * *

Write down the problem and any sub-issues, defining them as clearly as you can. Seeing them in black and white may help you to discern the limits of the problem and make it less daunting.

* * *

Break the problem down into its tiniest components, and tackle just one or two of these. Completing these tasks can give you the sense that you're making a little headway, and nudge you out of your paralysis.

* * *

For instant de-stressing, take some exercise, such as going for a brisk walk or run. The activity will lower your levels of stress hormones and raise your levels of endorphins (feel-good hormones), lifting your mood.

THE POWER OF QUESTIONS

When analyzing a problem, one of the best techniques is to ask lots of questions of yourself or other people. This can work because, in the past, you or others may have faced similar situations and come up with good solutions.

GETTING TO THE CRUX OF THE MATTER

Try analyzing your assumptions about a problem, and your ideas for solutions, by answering four basic questions:

- Why does this problem exist?
- Why do I see it as a problem?
- What would be the implications of using this solution?
- What would this solution give me that others wouldn't?

Use these questions to break your problem down into its fundamental elements. For example, if your issue is whether or not to buy a new car, you might start by asking yourself: "Why do I want a car?" Three of the possible answers might be:

- a need for transport to work
- a desire for greater freedom
- a yearning for a status symbol.

So, rather than defining your problem as "I want a new car", your real issue could become "I want a better way to get to and from work" or "I want a greater sense of freedom in my life".

By stripping back your problem to this basic level, you bring into play more options for finding solutions. Rather than restricting yourself to aiming for a new car, if you redefine your goal as, for example, "finding better transport for work", this may open up further considerations such as taking taxis, buses or trains, buying a bicycle, getting a lift from a work colleague, and so on.

ANALYSIS BY QUESTIONING

When next thinking of how best to tackle a particular problem or achieve a certain goal:

- ask yourself, "What is my underlying reason or need?"
- brainstorm other ways of meeting that need (see page 30)
- look at the options you've come up with during your brainstorming session: are any of these solutions better, easier or more appropriate than your original idea?

By using questioning in this way you may avoid pursuing an overly grandiose goal or following a time-consuming course of action when a far simpler solution would have sufficed.

"If you don't know, ask. You will be a fool for the moment, but a wise man for the rest of your life."

Seneca (4BC–AD65)

DIFFERENT TYPES OF THINKING

There are several forms of logical reasoning that you can use in problem-solving or decision-making. The options you consider, and the conclusions you reach, can vary greatly depending on which of them you apply. Here are a few common types of reasoning, with their benefits and pitfalls.

INDUCTION

Drawing general conclusions from the available evidence. The following famous example was given by philosopher of science Karl Popper, in the 1930s:

"I have only ever seen white swans, so I conclude that all swans are white."

Many forms of statistical sampling are based on this type of reasoning. However, the weakness of this mode of thinking is that you cannot use it to prove anything to be true, but merely to assert its likelihood. As Popper pointed out in this context, it would only take one sighting of a black swan to prove the conclusion false!

DEDUCTION

Drawing a conclusion logically implied by the propositions from which you started. As long as your starting facts are correct, your deductive conclusions will always be correct.

For example:

"My keys are definitely in the house or the car. I've searched the car:
therefore they must be in the house."

The pitfall is that you may place too much confidence in your starting
facts: can you be sure your keys are only in one of these two places?

PATTERN-MATCHING

Applying reasoning from past situations to new ones that seem
similar. As with induction, experts use this type of reasoning to find
rapid answers based on their wealth of experience. For example:

A doctor sees a patient with a red, swollen face and, on the basis of
past knowledge, diagnoses mumps.

While this method of reasoning can be lightning-fast, it depends on
clear and accurate perceptions. It is best used only when dealing with
situations that are very like those previously encountered, and where
the chances of coming across some new aspect are slim.

CHECK YOUR FACTS

Faulty reasoning can lead to poor decisions, so it's important always
to question how you reached a conclusion, and whether all the logical
steps you've applied actually bear up under scrutiny. The following
pages illustrate some traps into which faulty thinking can lead you.

THOUGHT WELLS ... AND HOW TO ESCAPE THEM

It's easy to believe that we always approach issues logically. Yet in fact our reasoning is often fallible: we may fall into traps, or "thought wells", from which we cannot escape. Being aware of common thought wells, and knowing how to avoid them or climb out, can greatly enhance our thinking.

THOUGHT WELL 1: DENIAL OR AVOIDANCE

Refusing to deal with unpleasant facts, either by denying that there's a problem or by avoiding the action needed to manage that problem.

- **Example** You're sinking into debt, yet you deny there's any problem – or, while accepting that the problem exists, you avoid taking practical steps to sort out your finances.

- **Escape route** This thought well is appealing if confronting or engaging with the truth scares you. To avoid it, remind yourself that, however bad it may feel to face reality, denial and avoidance are likely to cause you even greater pain. Ruthlessly reappraise all the facts. Make the task less disagreeable by rewarding yourself with small treats immediately after tackling it.

THOUGHT WELL 2: YES, BUT ...

Coming up with a variety of reasons, however spurious, why a new idea won't work, instead of exploring its possibilities.

- **Example** Friends invite you on a skiing holiday that you know you'd enjoy, yet your mind brings up a string of objections. "Who'll feed my cat?", "Suppose I make a fool of myself on the slopes!"
- **Escape route** Use the PIN approach:
  First, list everything **P**ositive about the idea.
  Now identify anything **I**nteresting, even if not especially positive.
  Finally, consider any **N**egative aspects or consequences.
  This PIN approach enables you to accentuate the positive aspects and remove or minimize any negatives. Put each negative to the test by questioning yourself: Is this *really* true? What evidence do I have that proves it?

THOUGHT WELL 3: GROUPTHINK

Automatically accepting the opinions of others – society, friends, family, colleagues – without first checking whether or not their assumptions are correct.

- **Example** Almost any statement beginning with something like "Everyone knows that ...", "All right-minded people agree ...", "It's common knowledge that ..."
- **Escape route** Assume nothing, question everything. Ask, "How do I really know?" rather than accepting things without hesitation. Consider the evidence in front of you before you rely on other people's view about "how things really are".

THOUGHT WELL 4: SELECTIVE VISION

Trying to make the facts of a situation conform to your previously reached conclusions.

- **Example** You see someone you love or admire through rose-tinted spectacles, and therefore everything they do is right. This blinkered view can apply to objects and organizations, too: an antiques dealer who wants to believe she has found a rare piece may be "blind" to any dubious characteristics, or shareholders may not question a reputable company's dealings.
- **Escape route** To bring some objectivity to your judgments, try actively looking for aspects that contradict the view you hold. Remember that selective vision works both ways: beware of seeing only the faults in someone or something, too.

THOUGHT WELL 5: A ONE-TRACK MIND

Refusal to recognize any need for new thinking. People tend to find it difficult to reverse a decision once made, or abandon a course of action they've begun, even if they come to realize it was a mistake.

- **Example** Denial by US motor manufacturers that Americans would ever be willing to buy compact cars.
- **Escape route** Regularly and stringently reappraise all your key assumptions. Never take anything for granted. A good strategy is to play "devil's advocate" with yourself. Can you spot the weak spots before anyone else does? What are you going to do about them? Be willing to consider reversing decisions if necessary: this is a sign not of weakness, but of adaptability.

THOUGHT WELL 6: OVER-COMPLICATING MATTERS

Ignoring the simplest explanation or solution in favour of an overly complex or less likely one.

- **Example** You can't find an item in your house and you assume that a burglar has stolen it rather than considering that you've simply misplaced it.
- **Escape route** Employ the principle of Occam's Razor – the rule that states: "All things being equal, the simplest solution is the best one."

THOUGHT WELL 7: NOT MY IDEA!

Dismissing an idea just because someone else thought of it.

- **Example** Your children refuse to do something they usually wouldn't mind doing, simply because you suggested it!
- **Escape route** Suggest actions in a way that lets the other person believe they thought of it first, or that allows them to adopt the suggestion as their own. If you're the one feeling uncomfortable with someone else's idea, remind yourself that the intelligent course of action is to adopt ideas on their own merits, not depending on who came up with them. You could also try adapting the idea by adding your own twist to it, so that it feels more like your own.

THE BABY ELEPHANT EFFECT

The decisions we make are built on a range of existing beliefs and assumptions. But if some of these assumptions are inaccurate, they may artificially constrain us into following non-existent rules or lead us to believe we have fewer options than is truly the case.

WHAT HELD THE ELEPHANT BACK?

There was once a baby circus elephant who, when not performing in the big top, was kept restricted to a small area by a chain attached to a stake. Although, when he was fully grown, the elephant could easily have broken the chain or pulled up the stake, he never attempted to do so. Why? When he was too small and weak to pull up the stake or break the chain, escape had been impossible, and this sense of what is called "learned helplessness" stayed with him throughout his life.

Similarly, we can often become blocked in our own thinking by assuming the presence of restrictions that don't actually exist. Like the baby elephant, we may have encountered such restrictions in the past and assume that they still apply.

MISGUIDED ASSUMPTIONS

The following puzzles are fun, but they also serve a serious purpose: to alert you to the ways in which false assumptions can lead you astray or prevent you from seeing all the possible options. The answers and explanations are on page 58.

The three links

A man has bought four gold chains that he wants joined together into a necklace for his wife. However, he can only afford for the jeweller to break and re-join three links. How could this be done?

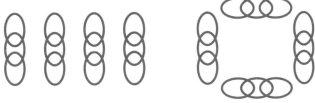

The cross of coins

Move just two of the coins from their positions below in order to create a cross of equal length and height, containing all the coins.

1	2	3	4
5	6	7	8
9	10	11	12
13	14	15	16

The number square

Place your pencil on the number 1 and, without lifting it off the page, draw a continuous line through every square, finishing in square 16. You may enter each square only once.

The three links

Position three of the chains in a triangle formation, then undo the three links of the remaining chain. Each of the three broken links can now connect the corners of the triangle. Thinking that the four chains need to be laid out in a square formation before being joined together is a false assumption.

The cross of coins

The solution here involves placing one coin on top of the middle coin. Many people find this puzzle hard because they assume that all the coins have to be placed side by side.

The number square

The clue is in the instruction that you can *enter* each square only once. If you begin on square 1, this still leaves you the option to re-enter it once you have left it – a flexibility in interpretation that many people overlook.

1	2	3	4
5	6	7	8
9	10	11	12
13	14	15	16

TESTING QUESTIONS

A helpful exercise to test the accuracy of an assumption or belief is to subject it to the following three questions:

* * * * *

Is my belief illogical? Does it make sense? Does it stand up to questioning?

Is my belief extreme? Does it match an objective assessment of the facts? Am I being selective in my choice of evidence to support my view?

Is my belief inflexible? Am I assuming that unless a particular choice is made or option chosen, everything will be ruined?

* * *

Here is an example of how this questioning tactic might work.

You are thinking of changing your job and have identified your problem with your present job as feeling depressed and worthless. You believe this is because your boss doesn't like you. You might ask yourself:

Is my belief illogical? Does my boss really dislike me?

Is my sense of being disliked extreme? What firm evidence do I have?

Am I being inflexible? Do I believe my boss has to like me all the time for me to feel valued and happy?

The answers that you give may confirm your assumption or put it in a new light, opening up new options.

CHANGING CONTEXTS AND PASSING TIME

One important point to bear in mind is that the factors that influence your decisions may not stay the same forever. The picture is likely to alter with the passage of time, and problems can appear or disappear almost overnight because of changes in the background context.

STAYING ALERT TO CONTEXT CHANGES

List the ways in which the context of your situation could change. Which elements of your life or environment, if removed or modified, would totally alter the problem, and what would the implications of such changes be? Which elements of your situation would become more or less significant as a result?

Keep an eye on the horizon. What small elements that exist now have the potential to grow in size and influence in the future? Watch out especially for any elements that are subject to exponential growth (growth in size or extent that accelerates at an increasingly rapid rate, building on itself in a "snowballing" effect – like the growth of algae over a pond). Unlike the regular course of linear growth, exponential growth can quickly alter the whole environment.

Because many actions can take months, years or even decades to show their full effects, the ultimate consequences of what we do, or fail to do, can be hard to predict or plan for. One major example is the threat of climate change: how are our activities today going to alter the world that we leave to our grandchildren?

CONTEXT CHANGES

The following examples illustrate how a change in the context of an issue can make a formerly pressing problem almost irrelevant, or cause completely new concerns to arise.

*   *   *   *   *

In technology
Imagine being a director at *Encyclopaedia Britannica* during the 1980s and worrying about soaring printing costs. You couldn't have known that within a decade your business would be revolutionized by the introduction of cheap CD-ROMs, making printing costs almost irrelevant.

*   *   *

In science
During the 1970s many scientists expressed concern over the likelihood of global cooling, but today they're concerned about global warming.

*   *   *

In demographics
Not long ago, many European nations were worried about over-population. Today they're even more concerned that falling birth rates will make it impossible to maintain a sufficiently young and vigorous workforce to support an ageing population.

*   *   *

In the media
Until recently, gigantic media corporations regulated the output of news. Many people became concerned about the extensive control that these organizations had over information. Now, with the growth of the internet, anyone can upload news or images, and people are becoming worried about the fact that nobody seems to be regulating this material.

WILL THIS GO ON FOREVER?

Estimating how long a situation will last can often affect how you view that situation and any decisions you take regarding it. If you knew, for example, that there was a better than even chance that your unpleasant new neighbours would move away within two years, that could affect how you decide to handle an ongoing dispute with them. But is it feasible to predict how long things will last?

An interesting perspective on this problem was devised by American physicist J. Richard Gott. In 1969, Gott visited the Berlin wall (built in 1961) and wondered how long it would remain standing. As there was nothing special about the time he'd picked to visit it, he reasoned that, if he could divide the wall's lifetime into four quarters, there was a 50 per cent chance that he was somewhere in the middle two quarters. Based on this assumption, he reckoned that there was a 50 per cent chance the wall would last from one-third to three times as long as it had already (more than two and two-thirds but less than 24 years). The wall was actually demolished 20 years later, in 1989.

Gott also estimated that there was a 95 per cent chance humanity would continue to exist for another 5,100 to 7.8 million years. The huge range results from his seeking such a high probability. The greater the certainty required, the wider the time span will need to be.

PICK A TIME, ANY TIME ...

You can use the Duration Calculator shown opposite, based on Gott's formula, to predict approximately how long an object or situation will last, without needing to know anything other than your subject's age.

For the calculation to work, there should be nothing special about the starting point. You can't, for example, use it to predict the length of a friend's marriage *at the time of the wedding*, because you're at a predetermined point: the start. Neither is it realistic for things that have a well-established average duration, such as a human life.

The calculation also works best on shorter time spans. With time that runs into decades or even longer periods, you can only produce impracticably broad estimates.

Some further examples for which this method can be applied include:
- How much longer is your car likely to keep running?
- How long might the company you work for last?
- (and one for fun) How long will the current number 1 book/film/single stay at the top?

While not amazingly accurate, the technique can certainly provide a different view that could influence your decision-making.

THE DURATION CALCULATOR

This calculation will give you a quick estimate of how long an object or situation might last, with a 60 per cent chance of being correct – better than evens, and without producing an unworkably broad time span.

Take the time (in weeks, months or years) that your object or situation has already been in existence.
- Multiply by 4 to give the longest time left.
- Divide by 4 to give the shortest time left.

MAKING YOUR DECISION

Being decisive and being effective go hand in hand. Once you've generated as many options as you can, considered them, and examined all the different angles, you should have all the necessary information on which to base a decision. This chapter covers some powerful and precise techniques for helping you to assess different options.

Making your decision also involves assessing risks. Everyone has a different attitude toward risks, and this chapter has exercises that help you to identify your own approach. There are also tips on eliminating common biases that can colour your thinking, and on getting the best from other people's input.

WEIGHING UP CHOICES

When you reach the stage in decision-making where you're confronted with more than one possible option, you need to make a choice. The next few pages show several techniques that can help you to weigh up one option against another.

PROS AND CONS

One of the founding fathers of America, Benjamin Franklin, invented perhaps the most famous method for making decisions. Simply list all the positive (pro) and negative (con) points for each option. Seeing them written down helps you to sort out their relative importance. You can go further: give each pro or con a score, and then add them up to give a total score for each option. (See pages 70–71.)

LIKELIHOOD vs DESIRABILITY

A more precise way to weigh up the relative attractiveness of your various options is to rate the possible outcome of each according to two factors: how likely it is and how desirable it is.

1   Give each option a mark out of 100, based on your estimate of the likelihood of a particular outcome. 0 would be "almost impossible", 50 represents an equal chance of the event happening or not happening, and 100 is "almost inevitable".
2   Then, rate how desirable the outcome of an option is on a scale of −7 to +7 (0 is neutral).

3   Multiply these two figures together (likelihood × desirability) to give a figure for the attractiveness of that option.

Attractiveness rating is most useful for comparing options for which the pros and cons are finely balanced: the outcomes might be desirable *but not* likely, or undesirable *but* likely.

For example, suppose you need to find a speaker quickly for a charity dinner. Sending out multiple requests could result in more than one acceptance, which would be embarrassing. The table below shows how you might work out the attractiveness of three choices, based on the likelihood of their being available and their desirability.

	Gloria Starlet	Marty Millionaire	Senator Wiseman
Likelihood	70	30	80
Desirability	3	6	-1
Attractiveness	210	180	-80

You could plot the results of your own comparative ratings for different options on an attractiveness scale like the one below.

The attractiveness scale

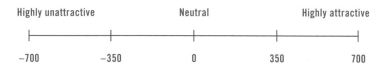

Highly unattractive   Neutral   Highly attractive

−700   −350   0   350   700

DECISION TREES

A decision tree is a diagrammatic method of showing what different courses of action could mean for you. Decision trees are a little like solution trees (see page 42), but rather than drawing out possible solutions, they are a way for you to plot alternative outcomes.

PLOTTING A DECISION TREE

Each decision you take opens up further possibilities. By plotting the course of these choices in the form of a diagram with branches, you can instantly see the relationship between the decisions and the outcomes they might yield. As an example, imagine that you're the head of a company, and you have the option of hiring a brilliant sales director who may or may not have committed fraud; the decision tree opposite outlines some possible choices, courses and outcomes.

The tree's two main branches represent the two choices: to employ the sales director or not. The twigs growing from each branch show the main consequences of each choice.

If you employ him, he may turn out to have been a fraudster, or he may not. Even if he *was* a fraudster, there are two possible consequences: he will defraud you, or he won't (two further twigs).

If you decline to employ the sales director, then the consequences are either that nothing will change (i.e. you will go on as before) or that another rival company will employ him and pose even greater competition for your firm than before.

COMPARING POSSIBLE OUTCOMES

Each consequence has been given a likelihood (L) and a desirability (D) rating, as described on pages 66–7. Note: the likelihood ratings for each major branch of your tree should add up to 100.

For each possible outcome, multiply the likelihood number by the desirability number to give an overall rating. (For example, the overall rating for "he defrauds you" would be 25×-7, giving −175.)

Finally, add up all the overall ratings for each of the two courses of action, in order to compare one total score against another.

In this example, the total on the "employ him" side is 300 (−175 + 125 + 350), and on the "decline him" side, −250 (−250 + 0), so the "employ him" option is clearly better. However, if the ratings had been different — say, if the likelihood of the man being a fraudster was higher — "decline him" could end up with a higher total score.

Decision tree

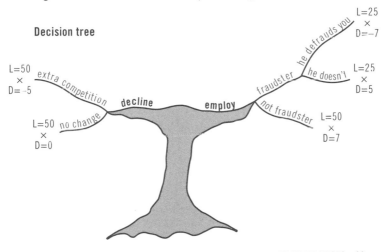

EFFORT AND REWARD

Another way to explore a range of options and decide which goal to pursue is to look at the ease of each task versus the possible rewards from the outcomes. There is a useful method of weighing up one goal against another in this way, based on a military technique called the CARVER matrix.

ADAPTING THE CARVER MATRIX

The original CARVER matrix was designed to help a military force assess which of a range of enemy targets it would be best to aim for. However, you can employ the technique for everyday purposes, to help you choose which of several options might be the best one to pursue.

CARVER is an acronym for:

Criticality: how vital is it to pursue this goal?

Accessibility: how easy is it to reach the goal?

Recognizability: how easy will it be for you to obtain information on how to achieve your goal, and to recognize when you are on target to achieve it?

Vulnerability: is your target easy to hit? The less force or energy it would take to overcome this challenge, the greater its vulnerability.

Effect: how much of an effect on your life, overall, would accomplishing this goal have?

Recuperability: if you fail to reach the goal, how much of a setback would the lost time and energy represent?

USING THE MATRIX

Draw up a grid like the one below, with a list of possible goals down the left-hand side and each point of the CARVER matrix across the top. If one of the criteria is not relevant to any of your particular range of goals, you can leave it out.

Then, for each goal, consider each of the six CARVER points and award them a score of −7 to +7. Pay special attention when rating V(ulnerability) and R(ecuperability). For each of these aspects, if they would require a lot of energy to achieve, you should give them a low rating (because any setback would involve a major loss of energy, which is undesirable), but if they involve little energy (and therefore little cost if you should fail), then give them a high rating.

Working along each row, add up the CARVER points for each goal. Write the total at the end of the row.

In the example shown here, Richard has reached a crossroads in his career and needs to decide which of three options to pursue: to take early retirement, to change companies or to go after his boss's job. His matrix ends up looking like this:

	C	A	R	V	E	R	Totals
Retire	-4	5	7	5	-1	3	15
Change job	5	2	3	2	7	-5	14
Boss's job	4	-1	6	3	6	-2	16

According to the matrix, going for the boss's job, with a total score of 16, is the best decision for Richard to pursue.

YOUR DECISION-MAKING STYLE

As well as assessing practical factors, such as likelihoods and benefits, you need to take account of your personal response to situations. Your outlook, and in particular your appetite for risk, can have a major bearing on your decisions.

HOW DO YOU HANDLE RISKS?
Imagine yourself in each of the following situations and think how you'd react. Then turn to pages 74–5 to find out your risk-taking style.

Situation 1
A friend gives you tips on three high-risk but high-yield shares. You make an excellent profit on the first, so you take that and invest it in the second, which also makes an excellent profit. Do you then ...

A place all your profits on the third tip?

B quit while you're ahead and not risk the third tip?

C place half your profits on the third – because you could make more, but if you don't, you've still got some left?

Situation 2
It's a fine, warm day, but the forecast warns of rain later. You're going to be walking a lot and will be carrying a briefcase and laptop, so an umbrella will be awkward and a raincoat will make you hot. Do you ...

A leave umbrella and coat behind, giving yourself less to carry and taking a chance that the fine weather will continue?

B take umbrella *and* raincoat, as it's better to be safe than sorry?

C just take the umbrella because, although it will be extra to carry, it will give you some protection if the heavens open?

Situation 3

You run a popular sandwich shop. The owner of a local business has provisionally promised you an order to supply all of his employees with their daily lunches, provided that you could start quickly. However, to meet this demand you would need to employ more staff, yet if the order doesn't materialize, you could be left in debt. Do you ...

A employ an extra person straight away so that you'll be in a position to take on the contract immediately, if you get it?

B wait until you have a signed contract before employing anyone?

C hire a temporary employee so that you could at least make a start on fulfilling the contract, but without having to risk the expense of taking on a full-time employee?

Situation 4

You need to sell your house quickly because you're moving to a new city, and paying to rent somewhere until you sell would cost you a lot of money. Someone makes you an immediate, unnegotiable offer, but it's less money than you wanted. Do you ...

A reject the offer in the hope that a better one will come soon?

B accept the offer immediately?

C try to keep the buyer interested, but stall for time in the hope that a better offer will appear?

WHAT YOUR ANSWERS MEAN

If you gave more A answers than B or Cs, then you're a Gambler.
If you gave more B answers than A or Cs, then you're a Banker.
If you gave more C answers than A or Bs, then you're an Investor.

Gambler

Gamblers tend to have an appetite for the highest gains, and
are willing to take the necessary risks to get them. They have an
entrepreneurial attitude toward life, and are always optimistic
about their chances of success.

Advice for gamblers:
- Check your facts (don't be a victim of too much optimism).
- Take out good insurance to safeguard against large losses.
- Make sure that you don't fall prey to the Gambler's Fallacy
  (see page 81).

Gambler　　　　Investor　　　　Banker

Banker

Bankers take the opposite view, and are usually highly averse to risk – avoiding loss is their main concern. Bankers are good at keeping a level head in risky situations, and at slow, steady growth over time.

Advice for bankers:

- Don't be blind to opportunities.
- Take care not to be too slow in analyzing situations that require speedy responses.
- Remember the maxim that we are more likely to regret the things that we didn't do than those that we did.

Investor

Investors take a middle-of-the-road position, attempting to compromise between risk and security. Essentially, investors want to minimize regret by avoiding the risk of big losses, while also trying to pursue opportunities. Investors are good in uncertain situations.

Advice for investors:

- Because you adopt a strategy halfway between those of the other two types, take into account the advice given for both.
- Beware of sitting on the fence or getting paralyzed by indecision.

To make the most of your own decision-making style, bear in mind its pros and cons. For certain situations, you may even find it helpful to consider an approach that's different from your normal style.

UNDERSTANDING RISK

When trying to judge risk, we don't always think rationally. We have certain responses programmed into our brains by evolution, allowing us to make decisions without having to wait for all the facts. These rules served us well in prehistory, but can all too easily lead us astray in the modern world.

FACTS vs FEELINGS

You should be able to assess any risk accurately provided that you have sufficient information. Such assessment is what insurance companies do by gathering data relating to the likelihood of an event.

However, every risk also has an emotional aspect: how risky you *feel* it to be. Emotional reactions form the basis of some misleading "rules of thumb", of which the five most frequent are listed below.

	We over-estimate the risk of, or are irrationally afraid of, threats that:	We under-estimate the risk of, or are unduly complacent about, threats that:
1	are new and/or rare	we are familiar with or that have been around a long time
2	other people cause	have natural causes
3	are beyond our control or are imposed on us	we can control or that we choose
4	don't bring any benefits	bring benefits or rewards
5	are spectacular and/or dramatic	seem mundane in character

Given that such common misconceptions bias our thinking, even when operating below the radar of conscious awareness, it's hardly so surprising that most of us have a skewed idea of actual risk. For example, although we're statistically far more likely to die of food poisoning or in a vehicle accident than in a plane crash or a terrorist attack, we'll usually be more afraid of these dramatic though relatively improbable events. Planes seldom crash, but these accidents rate as a high risk in our minds because they match numbers 3, 5 and sometimes 2 on the left-hand side of the list.

INCREASING OBJECTIVITY
Simply by being aware of these misleading "rules of thumb", we can more easily avoid being tricked by them.

Whenever you're **avoiding** taking a risk, check through the items on the left-hand side of the chart opposite. If the reasons for your feelings of threat involve one or more of those items, then think through whether your decision is rational and makes sense.

Alternatively, if you're going to be **engaging** in a risky activity, check your decision against the points listed on the right-hand side of the chart, to make sure that you haven't unreasonably downplayed the level of risk involved.

RISK vs BENEFIT
Another bias in how we think about risk is in our perception of losses and gains. Put simply, all other things being equal, if we're faced with a certain small loss, or a bigger but uncertain loss, we tend to

take the chance on the latter, even though this might not be prudent. However, when it comes to a gain, we prefer a guaranteed small gain over the chance of a possible bigger one.

The reasoning behind these apparently illogical biases probably arises from two common habits of thought. The "optimism bias" tends to make us believe that we're less likely to suffer loss than others. We also tend to place a higher value on rewards in the here and now than on those we might attain in the future, even if the latter are greater.

RELATIVE vs ABSOLUTE RISKS

A further factor that can bias our perception of risks is the absence of any point on which to base comparisons. For example, imagine if a new drug were shown to triple the chance that you'd develop a certain medical disorder as a side effect. The medicine, you might conclude, presented a high risk to you and therefore was not worth taking.

This is the risk as quoted in relative terms. However, the actual risk might be relatively low. If the chance of contracting the medical disorder were only 0.5 per cent to begin with, and rose to 1.5 per cent when you took the medication, this would indeed be a 300 per cent increase of risk in relative terms, but in absolute terms it would only amount to an extra 1 per cent chance of contracting the disorder.

CUMULATIVE vs ONE-OFF RISKS

As well as the relative or absolute level of risk, you also need to bear in mind the possible cumulative effect. Engaging in a low-risk activity regularly, over a long time, may pose a greater risk to you than engaging in a higher-risk activity once or just several times. (For example, smoking cigarettes may, in the long term, be more hazardous than bungee-jumping.) In particular, pay more attention to activities that appear to be low risk if they are one-off occurrences but add up to a larger risk over time, and that fall into one or more of the categories of under-estimated risks in the chart on page 76.

DESTINY – OR LUCK?

Millennia of evolution have turned the human brain into a finely tuned pattern-spotting device. So important was this skill to our ancestors that they would rather risk seeing patterns where there weren't any than miss possible signs of danger – the life-saving "those shadows might be a leopard" response. Today, however, this ingrained response may cause us to see patterns even where they don't exist.

Our brains leap at every chance to discern patterns, to perceive order in chaos, and this introduces an often subconscious bias into the way in which we assess risks and benefits. One of the most striking examples of this behaviour is in gambling, where people can interpret a succession of purely random events as evidence of a "lucky streak". This bias, and how to avoid it when deciding on a course of action, will be discussed next.

"Judgment comes from experience, and experience comes from bad judgment."

Simón Bolívar (1783–1830)

WHEN TO FLIP A COIN

Our view of risks and benefits is also influenced by our understanding, or misunderstanding, of chance. We have to be careful not to see a "run of luck" where none exists, but if we're finding it hard to make a simple either/or choice, then trusting to chance can be an effective course of action.

TRUE RANDOMNESS

Pick a number between one and ten. The chances are you picked an odd number, and it's most likely to be 7. Statistically, this is the most commonly chosen number. If people's choices were truly random, then an equal number would pick even numbers as pick odd numbers, and 1, 3, 5 and 9 would be as popular as 7. This simple test shows the inbuilt bias that can exist in our minds even when we make abstract choices that have little or no bearing on our welfare.

When you need to make a clear-cut choice between two equally attractive alternatives, the best strategy is to flip a coin. Remember: the chance of whether a coin lands on heads or tails remains 50:50 every time (presuming that the coin has not been tampered with).

Flipping a coin can also have a more subtle way of influencing your decision. Once you've flipped it, just before you look you'll almost certainly feel a pang of hope that it has landed on one side rather than the other! That reaction, rather than how the coin actually falls, will tell you which outcome you truly prefer – and, if necessary, you can then overrule the coin.

THE GAMBLER'S FALLACY

When faced with a random risk, such as the risk of losing money in a game of chance, people tend, incorrectly, to see winning or losing streaks, or anticipate that their "luck" is about to "change". This belief is known as the Gambler's Fallacy. Of course, in situations where the outcome might well depend on non-random factors, such as skill, reversals of fortune and winning and losing streaks may be meaningful concepts, but in any situation in which the risk is truly random, you must be careful not to fall for the Gambler's Fallacy!

THE RULE OF 30

How do you work out whether some particular results you are getting are due to chance or to some other factor, such as skill? Trying a particular course of action 30 times will give you a good indication. By having 30 goes at something you want to do (such as applying for a job) or getting 30 informed opinions on an idea, you have a way of gauging whether your decision has potential. Repeated runs of good or bad results will help you to discount any element of chance.

DICE LIVING

A surprise bestselling book in the 1970s, *The Dice Man* by Luke Rhinehart, triggered a craze for "dice living", in which people make key decisions on the basis of throwing dice. Its adherents claim it makes them feel more alive as it introduces a greater element of the unpredictable into their existence, and often gives them an excuse to do things they always wanted, without having to feel responsible for taking the decision.

GROUP DECISION-MAKING

Group decision-making combines the experience and intelligence of many people. This has its advantages and its drawbacks. The information below shows when it's appropriate to involve groups of people in decisions, and how you can get the best from them.

THE BENEFITS

Groups can often make better decisions than individuals. Indeed, intelligent behaviour in nature doesn't always come from single creatures – social insects, like ants, are individually simple-minded, but collectively display intelligent behaviour by working as a group.

Groups are less likely to miss out on information, as they have more eyes and ears than any one person, and individual errors at either extreme of their range of opinions tend to cancel each other out. This is particularly true for estimations of quantities or values (see box below). Market economies harness this power by effectively letting the consumers, rather than any central body, set the values of goods.

A REASONABLE AVERAGE
If you place a jar of jellybeans in front of a crowd and get each person to estimate (without knowing the others' guesses) how many jellybeans there are in the jar, the average of all the estimates typically turns out to be surprisingly accurate: the mistakes (the extremes in either direction) tend to cancel each other out.

THE DRAWBACKS

Deciding as a group removes or weakens the burden of responsibility from individuals. If you need responsibility to be taken for a task, try to assign it to one individual. For example, if you need emergency help in public, rather than just giving a general cry for help, try to make eye contact with a specific passer-by and address them directly.

This lessening of responsibility can lead group members toward extreme opinions. Psychologists call this the "risky shift" – the tendency for moderate group members to assume that fellow members hold a more extreme view and adjust their own view in that direction. "Conservative shifts" are also possible. Watch out for group opinions that are far more risky or conservative than your own.

Creative activities, such as designing a building or making a movie, can be performed well by groups – but there's a danger of "design by committee", leading to a mish-mash of dull compromises. It's best to have one person guiding the activity. For example, if your office needs a new interior design, you might get the staff to set the brief for the work and decide who has the best flair for design, and then leave the chosen person to make the creative decisions.

COMPETITION AND GAME THEORY

Head-to-head competition with others uses up energy that you need for pursuing your goals. A more effective approach is to work out other people's likely actions and fit your response to them. This strategy has been studied in a branch of maths called game theory; three aspects are given here.

WHERE POSSIBLE, SEEK TO COOPERATE

Often, competition results in an "arms race" in which both sides are working as hard as possible just to keep up, yet neither ever gains an advantage over the other. Game theory predicts that, wherever possible, it's best to cooperate, and to form long-lasting, mutually beneficial relationships with those individuals and groups that are best at cooperating. However, if someone appears desperate to interact with you, it may be worth questioning whether you're actually getting the worse end of the deal!

FIND YOUR DOMINANT STRATEGY

You're shopping at the last minute for a birthday present for your mother. Your sister is also out buying a present and you're worried you might buy the same thing but you're unable to contact her. So you must make a choice. The two choices are: a specific perfume or a new skirt. If you and your sister both bought a skirt, your mother would be able to take one back for a refund. If you both chose the perfume, you know the shop wouldn't issue a refund. Therefore, no matter what your sister does, buying the skirt is your dominant strategy – it's your best course of action, regardless of what she's doing.

ELIMINATE THE WEAKEST STRATEGIES

In situations where there seems to be no clear dominant strategy for you to pursue, come at it from the opposite direction. Work out and eliminate what would be your weakest strategy, then your next weakest, and so on, until you arrive at the least weak strategy.

THE PRISONER'S DILEMMA

The police are holding a thief and his accomplice in separate cells. They offer one of them a deal: confess and you'll go free; don't confess and if your accomplice confesses, he'll go free and you'll receive a 10-year prison sentence; if you both confess, you'll each get a two-year sentence. Evidence is weak, and the prisoner knows that if he and his comrade both stay silent they'll only receive a six-month sentence. Here's how the prisoner can summarize his choices in a "payoff matrix":

	I stay silent	I confess
My accomplice stays silent	We both serve six months	I go free; he serves 10 years
My accomplice confesses	I serve 10 years; he goes free	We both serve two years

The ideal situation would be for both to stay silent, but if the prisoner can't trust his accomplice 100 per cent, then by staying silent he risks a 10-year sentence; therefore, his best option is to confess. This neatly illustrates how forming a cooperative allegiance is the best option.

INTERLUDE
LESSONS FROM THE PAST

History shows many examples of tragic and bad decisions, some of which have led to huge losses of life. However, along the way there have also been lesser blunders with a humorous side to them. Here are just a few, and the lessons we can learn from them.

MISSED OPPORTUNITIES

Steam power was known to the Romans, yet they never capitalized on its industrial potential. Instead, it was used as a novelty, with demonstrations of steam-powered door-openers and steam-powered horn-blowers. If they'd taken it more seriously, then the industrial revolution might have occurred almost two millennia earlier, and given the Romans wealth beyond their dreams. Some have argued that the easy availability of slave labour at the time blinded the Romans to the potential for steam-powered machines.

In 1667, the Dutch accepted a small spice island, called Pulau Run, from the British in exchange for Manhattan, an action which has been called "the worst deal in history". Spices, in particular nutmeg, were extremely profitable luxuries at the time, and Pulau Run, as almost the world's sole source of nutmeg, must have seemed like a great acquisition. However, the Dutch failed to take two facts into consideration: a Dutch commander, in an act of sabotage, had already landed on the island and cut down all the nutmeg trees; and secondly. nutmeg turned out to be fairly easy to grow elsewhere! Still, even though the British gained Manhattan, they were only able to hold on to it for a little over a century.

Lesson: Bad decisions can result from not realizing the true value of what you have.

FALSE PREPARATIONS

On the eve of the year 1000, many people in Europe believed that the end of the world was at hand. According to some accounts, they had spent the preceding months giving away their worldly possessions and engaging in self-mortification to prepare themselves for the afterlife.

We may laugh now, but the lead-up to the year 2000 arguably saw a folly on a far greater scale: the millennium bug panic. It was thought that computers' internal clocks would become confused once the years no longer began "19–", and would cause the computers to crash. Many have said – admittedly with hindsight – that the fantastic sums of money spent by governments and large companies to prepare for the threat were unnecessary. They point to the fact that for others, including small businesses, schools and even countries such as Italy, a lack of preparation had no harmful effect when the clock struck midnight on December 31, 1999. (See Understanding risk, page 76, on how we're more likely to fear threats that involve rare and dramatic factors, such as technological disasters.)

Lesson: Panic and fear of the unknown can lead to a frenzy of unnecessary work that achieves little.

OVERLOOKING DETAILS

In 1962, the first ever interplanetary spacecraft, Mariner 1, failed four minutes after take-off. Were it not for a replacement craft, Mariner 2, the incident could have put a premature end to NASA's interplanetary probe programme. The critical failure in the $80 million craft was a single missing hyphen in the software controlling it.

A similar, but even more expensive, mistake occurred years later, in 1999, on the launch of a Milstar military satellite. The craft misfired soon after launch and was placed into an incorrect and useless orbit. The problem resulted from a misplaced decimal point in the rocket's software. This tiny error resulted in the failure of a mission which had cost over $1 billion.

Lesson: If a small contribution or step towards a big goal is badly planned or omitted, it can jeopardize the whole outcome.

GROUPTHINK LUNACY

When the tulip was introduced into Europe in the mid-16th century, it soon became popular, with members of the upper classes vying to own the rarest specimens. By the early 17th century, competition for them in the Netherlands reached such heights that bulbs were being traded on the stock exchanges, and cost as much as the average Dutchman would earn in seven years. When the bubble burst in 1637, many were said to have lost everything they had through their avid speculation.

The "burst bubble" effect is particularly associated with a doomed venture almost a century later. The South Sea Company was granted a monopoly on trade with South America, and then later expanded its interests, taking on a large amount of government debt. The excitement of trade with the New World, combined with the security of a regular profit from government debt, drove investors into a frenzy. Shares in the company multiplied in value by ten times in the course of just a year. Soon after, the stock price collapsed, ruining many people. The event became known as the "South Sea Bubble". Sir Isaac Newton, who himself lost £20,000 in the Bubble, commented, "I can calculate the movement of the stars, but not the madness of men."

Lesson: The majority can be wrong. There's more about "groupthink" on page 53, and about group decision-making on pages 82–3.

HANDLING STRESS AND EMOTIONS

Many people assume that emotions are the opposite of the clear-headed rationality central to good decision-making. The truth, however, is that while our head and our heart can sometimes tug in different directions, mostly we use them both in concert whenever we make a decision. This chapter looks at how you can accentuate the best aspects of your emotional self, and boost positive feelings, to help you toward your goals. However, in some cases making new choices can push you outside your comfort zone and into new ways of behaving, which can cause anxiety, so the chapter also offers guidance on ways to cope with stress and negative emotions, such as worry.

DISCOVER YOUR TRUE TEMPERAMENT

Temperament refers to those parts of your personality governing emotional responses. Understanding more about your own deep-seated reactions to situations can help you to make the most of your personal qualities and overcome any mental blocks in making decisions or taking action.

INSIGHT INTO YOUR EMOTIONAL TRAITS

Your emotional responses are hard-wired into you: they depend on the sensitivity of your nervous system, and the degree to which your brain controls your reactions. The quick assessment on the opposite page will give you an insight into your own responses.

Rate each statement on a scale of 1 (hardly at all) to 7 (very true). Note your score in the white square of each row.

To obtain the most accurate score, take the assessment on three separate days, and then average the results by adding up your scores for each day and dividing by 3. In addition, bear in mind that, as an adult, your natural temperament can be obscured by other personality characteristics and by the demands of life and relationships, so try to imagine how you would have responded if you had taken the test when you were still a young child. Alternatively, ask three people who know you well to rate you, then average their results as before.

Your scores show where you fall on two scales that psychologists call traits. The number in the first column is your Body Excitability or BE score. The one in the second is your Cortical Inhibition or CI score.

	=BE	=CI
Sometimes I feel down or depressed for no good reason.		
I enjoy socializing.		
I often worry about things I've said or done in the past, and what impression these made on others.		
I'm easily irritated.		
People I've just met would say I'm a talkative person.		
My feelings are easily hurt.		
People I've just met would, generally, say I'm quite a lively person.		
I regularly have very strong emotional reactions, and find that my mood goes up and down during the space of a day.		
I'm able to let my hair down at a party.		
I thrive on meeting new people.		
Total up your scores in each column and divide each by 5		

Your **BE (Body Excitability)** score shows how sensitive your sympathetic nervous system is. A high score means that you are easily emotionally moved, while a low score means you are harder to excite.

Your **CI (Cortical Inhibition)** score refers to how strongly or weakly your cortex (the higher brain) inhibits your behaviour. In essence, a high score means that you're extroverted and fairly uninhibited; a low score means that you're shy, controlled and introverted. However, this score may depend, to some extent, on the situation you find yourself in: you might, for example, be quite outgoing among friends but more reserved at work or among strangers.

TRAITS AND TEMPERAMENT

By combining your trait scores from the previous page, you can see which of the four basic temperaments you have: sanguine, choleric, melancholic or phlegmatic. On the chart below, mark your trait scores on each line and then draw a straight line between the two marks. The quadrant your line crosses will indicate your temperament.

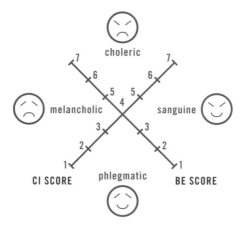

THE FOUR
TEMPERAMENTS

The main characteristics of each temperament are given below.
Each one has its advantages and drawbacks. In order to make the
best of your own temperament, follow the suggestions given here
to accentuate the positive aspects and minimize any weak points.

*   *   *   *   *

Sanguine Your outgoing, optimistic, stable nature helps you to deal
with most situations. However, you may rely too much on hunches
and assumptions, and misdirect your efforts. Harness your energy by
planning carefully (see page 115) and staying focused (see page 16).

*   *   *

Phlegmatic Calm, observant, steady but reserved, you're great at seeing
tasks through to the end, but may find it hard to assert yourself. Take
note of the NLP techniques on pages 108–9. You also tend to resist
action and change, so refer to the motivation advice on pages 116–17.

*   *   *

Melancholic Your naturally quiet exterior masks intense sensitivity.
Enhance your mood, and draw out your creativity, with uplifting music
and pleasant surroundings (see pages 106–7). You may need to control
a tendency to worry (see pages 100–101) or even panic (see page 47).

*   *   *

Choleric You are lively, hot-headed, outgoing and excitable. Your energy
and ability to make quick decisions are great assets. However, you need
to recognize when to think things through more carefully. To help control
any outbursts of emotion, refer to "When *not* to decide" (see page 103).

EMOTIONAL FORECASTING

Emotional reactions affect perception and judgment not only in actual situations, but also when we try to recall how we felt in the past or predict how we're likely to feel in the future. The following tips should help you to recognize and compensate for some common forms of emotional bias.

THE OVER-REACTION BIAS

People commonly over-estimate, and quite significantly, just how good or bad they'll feel in a particular situation. Researchers in one experiment asked people to predict how they'd feel if their favoured sports team won or lost a crucial match. The researchers rechecked their subjects' feelings just after the game, and then checked again several months later.

They found that not only did the spectators over-estimate how good or bad they'd feel about the results of the match, compared to how they reported feeling immediately after the game was over, but when asked again several months later, they once again over-estimated the intensity of their feelings at the time.

EMOTIONAL COLOURING

Another factor that can interfere with our ability to predict feelings accurately is that we're more likely to recall strong emotions than mild ones, even if the times of strong emotion were the exception. This means that if, even once, you felt very good or very bad in a particular situation, that one experience will colour your expectations of similar situations in the future more than it should.

MATERIALISTIC THINKING
A sure-fire way to make yourself unhappy is to compare yourself with people who are richer, more intelligent or more successful. Instead, follow the time-honoured advice to "count your blessings", and remember those who are less fortunate than yourself.

A materialistic view can also colour how you gauge the importance of a goal or the rightness of a decision. Some people assume that owning the latest must-have item, such as a new stereo or a car, will make them happier than it actually does. Even when people recognize this as a false expectation of happiness, they may still devote a lot of time and energy to attaining such items.

PREDICTING FEELINGS MORE ACCURATELY
Being aware of how recollections and expectations often play us false can help you to avoid falling into these traps. When considering any course of action, remember the following points:
- One bad experience shouldn't put you off trying again.
- Not all holidays, parties or other good times will be as great as the best you ever had.
- Material goods are unlikely to make you as happy as you expect.

If you're not sure how you'll cope in an unknown situation, ask someone actually in that situation how *they* do it.

THE ROLE OF SELF-ESTEEM

Many people mistakenly equate self-esteem with self-love, but it has more to do with developing qualities that enable you to respect yourself. Self-esteem also involves taking responsibility for your life. It can give you the confidence you need to tackle challenges and reach your goals.

THE SIX TENETS OF SELF-ESTEEM

The psychologist Nathaniel Branden was one of the pioneers of research on self-esteem. He identified six tenets of strong self-esteem, which you need to practise in everyday life.

- **Living consciously** This means striving to be aware at all times, taking actions appropriate to a situation, and not denying reality.
- **Self-acceptance** See your good and bad points just as they are. Even if there are some points that you want or need to change, start by accepting all of them as a fact.
- **Self-responsibility** This involves taking charge of your own life. If you avoid such responsibility, you deny yourself a source of power.
- **Self-assertiveness** Would you trust a friend who never stood up for you? If you treat yourself like this, you lose self-respect.
- **Living purposefully** If you have ambitions or goals, and apply self-discipline to achieve them, you'll feel better about yourself.
- **Personal integrity** Would you trust someone who breaks promises and tells lies? It can be tempting to do these things if you think no one else will know – but you're only betraying yourself.

BUILDING SELF-ESTEEM

One way to enhance your self-esteem, and help yourself to grow as a person, is to try the following exercise, devised by Dr Branden. It's based on the idea that it's easier to make tiny (5 per cent) changes often than to try big (100 per cent) changes all at once.

In this technique, you write down a "sentence stem" and complete the sentence with your own idea. For example:

If I were to bring 5 per cent more consciousness to my life …
… I would listen more carefully to what people are saying.

Create your own sentence stems for each of the tenets listed opposite. In each case, try to complete ten sentences from one stem. Do it as quickly as you can to let ideas bubble up from the subconscious.

SELF-ESTEEM BOOSTERS
Here are some more tips to help you increase your confidence, purpose and sense of your own capabilities.

- Think of your favourite activity, and remember what it was like to try it for the first time. Remind yourself that it's only natural to feel unsure of yourself when you're stepping outside your comfort zone.
- List all the things you've learned or achieved in the past 10 years.
- Go and do something you're good at, no matter how small.
- Complete a small task that you've been putting off.
- Shift the focus off yourself and your flaws. Do something to occupy your mind and preferably get it into the "peak" state (see page 104).

CONQUERING WORRY

Everyone's plagued with worries at times. While you need to be cautious when making important decisions, worry is a misuse of the imagination, which can blight your perception and kill your confidence. However, it is possible to control worries, to leave your mind free for effective action.

WORRY-ZAPPING STRATEGIES

When we worry, our minds tend to fixate on all sorts of dreadful outcomes, no matter how unlikely – a process that psychologists call "awfulizing". Worrying also tends to be unproductive, as it causes us to become paralyzed by a problem rather than focusing on a solution. We can get caught up thinking the same thoughts over and over, and dwelling on things that we don't have the power to change, such as decisions or actions we took in the past.

The American theology professor Haddon W. Robinson once wrote: "What worries you, masters you." If you find yourself suffering from excessive worrying, try some of these worry-zappers.

Break your worry down

Ask yourself: "Why am I worried?" Try to come up with as clear an answer as possible. Next, ask: "Is it reasonable to be worried about this issue?" or "What do I find so particularly bad about this issue?" Try to identify any sub-issues that you need to think about. Once you have identified these issues, it should be easier to tackle them.

Nip worries in the bud

Worrying is often linked to procrastination. While, in certain circumstances, delay can be a constructive strategy (see page 103), letting a situation drag on can also allow worries to accumulate. Like weeds shooting up in a garden, worries are far easier to deal with if you tackle them as soon as they appear, and don't allow them to grow deep roots in your mind.

Decide on an action

The more you put off making a decision or taking action, the more likely you are to fret endlessly about possible horrendous outcomes. If you're feeling paralyzed with worry, try to take some initial step toward tackling your problem, even if it's only a tiny one – you should find it easier going once you've made a start.

Mentally accept the worst

Make the best and most detailed plan you can think of for what you would do if the worst possible outcome occurred. Having prepared your worst-case scenario, tell yourself that there's no point in thinking about this issue any further.

Distract yourself

Worries have the best opportunity to consume your thinking when you have a lot of time on your hands. If you find yourself worrying when you're bored, immediately distract yourself with another task, no matter what, to break your train of thought.

Change your body language

Worrying can make you feel depressed. Counteract this low mood by adopting positive, confident body language. Stand tall. Unfold your arms to open your body. Raise your head and pull your shoulders back. The more confident your posture, the more confident you'll feel.

Don't bottle up your worries

Simply telling someone else about your worries or writing them down can usually make you feel less concerned.

BANISHING SELF-DOUBT

Worrying about your own ability to achieve a goal or solve a problem can become a self-fulfilling prophecy: if you lose confidence and self-belief, you'll be less able to do what you need to do. Using the strategies for boosting self-esteem (see pages 98–9) can help you to minimize or even banish worries of this kind.

TACKLING EXTERNAL PROBLEMS

Worries of the external kind, which you feel have been imposed upon you, are often actually problems that need to be solved, and the worry stems from not being able to influence these external factors. Try the questions on pages 48–9 to help you get to the heart of the issue, and see pages 40–45 for different ways to analyze problems.

See also pages 104–5 for advice on achieving the right amount of mental stimulation, between the extremes of panic and boredom, that will provide you with the energy to tackle your worries.

WHEN *NOT* TO DECIDE

Always make sure you're feeling clear-headed and confident before making any major decision. Physical or emotional stress can result in mistakes. If you know you're currently not up to dealing with an issue, it's best to leave it and revisit it when you feel stronger.

*   *   *   *   *

Avoid making decisions ...

When feeling tired – Napoleon was reported to have said he'd "never met an officer with 3am courage". Everything seems worse in the middle of the night, when your energy is at its lowest ebb. Try to get some sleep (or a 10-minute daytime nap) to refresh your mind.

When feeling overly worried – first deal with the emotions stirred up by worry (see pages 100–102).

When feeling angry or upset – take time to cool off first. If you're talking to someone else and they get upset, suggest a brief "time out".

When not clear-headed – even a single alcoholic drink or dose of medication can impair your decision-making abilities.

When feeling low – if you're feeling hopeless about a situation, check to see if hunger, illness or stressful surroundings might be adding to your woes. Look after yourself, and take action when you feel better.

A STATE OF BALANCE

We perform at our best in a state called the "zone of optimal mental achievement", when a task is finely balanced between being too easy or boring, and too difficult or stressful. Psychologists also refer to this state as "flow".

A ZONE OF OPTIMAL MENTAL ACTIVATION

When we're in the zone of optimal mental achievement, or "flow", we're able to work harder and longer, are more focused and enjoy the task more. Time flies by as we become absorbed by what we're doing.

This fairly small zone is illustrated on the graph below. The curved line shows mental performance, with "boredom" at one extreme and "panic" at the other. The peak state is at the top of the curve. To track your own state, choose a regular task that you'd like to enjoy more or do better. Each time you've performed the task, sketch a copy of this graph, and place an X at the point you felt you were at. If you felt

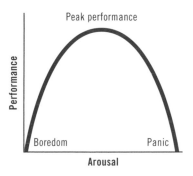

bored or indifferent, your X will be to the left of the peak; if you felt too stretched and stressed, it will be to the right. Repeat this step after several sessions, drawing a new graph each time so you're not influenced by your previous assessments. Evaluate your graphs: where are your Xs positioned most often?

Too many in the boredom region?

- Ask yourself: "If I were to be the best person in the world at performing this task, how would I do it?" Aim to become excellent.
- Could you get someone else to perform parts of the task that don't interest you, to enable you to spend more time on areas that do?

Too many in the panic region?

- Practice helps. Most people are able to shift out of the panic region as they become more practised and familiar with the activity or task.
- Ask for help: can you get others to give you a helping hand? Many "panic region" responses arise simply because you're trying to take on too much by yourself.
- If you feel you're far into the panic region, ask yourself whether the task is too hard for you at your current level of skill. Do you need more training or qualifications? Is the task itself too risky?
- Deal with anxiety by deep breathing. Place one hand on your chest and the other on your abdomen. Take slow, deep breaths, pulling the air right down into your lungs as you inhale. You should feel your abdomen moving more than your chest.

REDUCING STRESS AT WORK

Most modern workplaces are much safer than those of the past, yet these apparently benign environments are often contributing to chronic levels of stress. Here are some ways in which you can stay healthy and stress-free in the office.

STAY HYDRATED

Dehydration can sap your stamina and concentration. When you're preoccupied with work, it can be easy to ignore thirst, which is an early sign of the problem. Modern offices can also contribute to dehydration. Often, the air is dry, while the drinks typically on offer – tea, coffee and sugared soda drinks – relieve thirst but actually end up flushing more liquid out of your body. The most hydrating drink to have is water. Try to drink eight glasses of water a day. Take regular sips; don't wait until you're thirsty.

CREATE A NEGATIVE ION ATMOSPHERE

Ions (electrically charged atoms) in the atmosphere can affect your mood. Positive ions can make you feel tense, tired, achy and depressed, while negative ions can make you relaxed and happy. This is why offices often have an intangibly unpleasant feel: electronics and synthetic fabrics create an excess of positive ions in the air. Negative ions proliferate around moving water, such as the sea, rain, or waterfalls. You don't need moving water in your office, however: try placing an ionizer device (available from health shops) on your desk.

MAXIMIZE YOUR EXPOSURE TO NATURAL LIGHT

Scientific studies show that long-term exposure to artificial light can lead to physical and mental stress. Try using daylight-corrected bulbs, working near a window, and going outside whenever possible to expose yourself to natural light.

BENEFIT FROM GREENERY

Research has found that views of grass and trees reduce headaches, sore eyes and aching muscles, and induce a feeling of being wakefully relaxed. Even if you're in a city, adding pictures of rural views, having plants on your desk and taking walks in green spaces will give you these benefits.

PRACTICAL NLP TECHNIQUES

Taking action can mean casting off old beliefs and thinking in a new way. Until we become used to this, we will feel outside our "comfort zone". One approach to rethinking how we see things is NLP: neuro-linguistic programming.

THE BASICS OF NLP

Neuro-linguistic programming shows ways in which you can think more productively by changing the "language" of your thoughts: how you use words and create images and sensations in your imagination.

Here are three of the most powerful practical techniques from NLP, aimed at increasing flexibility in our thinking and perceptions.

Produce positive feelings at will

The power of association can switch on a specific emotion. Try this by thinking of a situation when you felt at your most confident, happy or decisive. Imagine it as vividly as you can. Make the feeling twice as intense, and then twice as intense again. At the same time, press the tips of your thumb and forefinger together. With practice, you'll only need to press your fingertips together to relive this positive feeling.

Change memories and beliefs

If you wish to take the sting out of a disagreeable memory, there are several steps you can take. Visualize it in black and white, and as a still rather than a moving image. Picture unpleasant people or things as smaller than they were. Imagine the scene from the position of another person, and then imagine the whole thing on a small TV screen, diminishing the importance of the memory.

You can enhance a good memory by doing the opposite: see it in vivid colours, and imagine living through it again. You can use a similar method to instil a new positive belief about yourself. Think of a good quality that you already have. How do you imagine yourself showing that quality? What colours, actions and sounds do you associate with it? Create your new belief using the same elements.

Model how you'd like to be
Just as children learn from role models, you can change your attitude or behaviour by "thinking yourself into" a person whom you wish to emulate in a particular respect. Close your eyes and imagine, in as much detail as you can, this person standing in front of you. Step into their skin and become them. How does their posture feel? Their emotional state? Their thoughts? What insights does this give you?

THE BACKGROUND OF NLP
NLP was invented in the 1970s by Richard Bandler and John Grinder. They studied the techniques of several eminent therapists, incorporating ideas from psychology, hypnotherapy and philosophy, and based the idea on modelling the thought and communication patterns of successful or well-adjusted people. Since then the field has exploded, with countless books, courses and CDs produced which use different forms of NLP. While some people have criticized the theories as unoriginal or even unscientific, many find NLP techniques useful.

CHAPTER 6

TAKING ACTION

Among the most valuable resources that you have are your time and energy, and this final chapter is all about deploying these precious assets effectively. It includes topics such as scheduling tasks, time management, maintaining motivation through the rough patches and focusing your efforts on the areas that really matter.

Decisions only become meaningful once they're translated into action. Together with all you've learnt so far, this chapter will equip you to follow your decisions all the way through, from a well-made plan to a satisfying conclusion.

SETTING GOALS

Goals help you to get things done. A clear aim, rather than a vague aspiration, will enable you to focus your efforts effectively, and will provide you with a real sense of achievement once you've reached your target.

THE POWER OF GOALS

Psychological research has shown that defining clear goals to work toward can greatly improve your performance in several ways:

- by directing your attention and actions
- by increasing the energy you put into a task
- by strengthening your persistence and tenacity
- by motivating you to find effective solutions for problems.

Goals that offer you a real challenge are much better for you than easy targets, or just trying to do your best. Choose a goal that will stretch you beyond your comfort zone. This will take you into your "peak" state (see page 104), when work is at its most satisfying and productive.

The only exception is if your goal is likely to be too hard for you at present and possibly push you into your "panic" zone. In that case, set yourself a series of intermediate "learning goals", each of which will be an achievement in itself but also a stepping stone toward your final goal. For example, if your goal is to give a presentation at work, practise by giving the talk to your mother, best friend or dog before stepping in front of that audience!

THE SMART APPROACH
A correctly formulated goal should be SMART:

Specific: it should be well defined.
Measurable: it should produce measurable results, so that you can
  track your progress.
Achievable: while challenging, a goal should still be, in theory, within
  your potential capabilities.
Rewarding: there needs to be some form of reward to motivate you to
  complete the goal (see pages 116–17).
Timed: it should have a deadline, as should any sub-goals.

WRITE IT DOWN
Give your goal a definite shape by writing it down. Keep this statement
in an easily accessible place – or even make it into a notice and
display it in a place where you'll see it all the time.

For a material goal, such as buying a house or negotiating a pay
rise, set a deadline for when you want to achieve it. For example: "By
December 31 next year I will own my own house."

If your goal is non-material, such as losing weight or becoming
more confident, write it down as though it is already happening. For
example: "I am becoming more and more confident each day."

Your subconscious doesn't understand the concept of a negative,
so always write goals in the positive:

I will lose weight   not   I won't eat any more chocolate

AN INITIAL REALITY CHECK

To help maximize your chance of eventual success, you need to make sure that your plans and actions will stay on track from the start. The best way is by testing your goal in the real world. To take an everyday example, if you're planning to paint your house, it would be sensible to buy a tiny "tester" pot of paint and try it out on an unobtrusive area first. A quick initial test will help to minimize the cost of failure and add to your knowledge. It will also make your emotional forecasting more realistic, and ward off the biases that could otherwise creep in once you've embarked on a course of action, such as faulty emotional forecasting (see pages 96–7) and a one-track mind (see page 54).

If it will take a long time for the full effects of your goal to become apparent, do as much preliminary testing as possible. For example, if you're thinking of starting the long and expensive training to become an architect, you might test your decision by getting work experience in an architect's office, to find out if you're likely to enjoy the job.

CREATING AN
ACTION PLAN

The more difficult, challenging or complex a project is, the more thought and planning you'll need to do at the outset to enable it to run smoothly. Here are some tips for drawing up an action plan.

* * * * *

1 Define your ultimate aim as clearly as you can: submit it to the SMART test (see page 113).

2 What kind of task is it: convergent (with just one or a few possible solutions), or divergent (with a wide range of possibilities)? See pages 40–44 for tips on dealing with each type.

3 If you're dealing with a "divergent" situation (the more common type), try to narrow down your options by using the attractiveness scale (see page 67) or the CARVER matrix (see page 71). Draw up a solution tree (see page 42) to work out the steps toward your goal.

4 Set a deadline.

5 List all the elements or stages of your project. Draw up a variable timeline (see pages 122–4) based on these elements, to give yourself a clear schedule to work to.

6 Are any other people going to be involved in your project? If so, brief them on their role.

7 Prepare for your first move and make a start!

BOOSTING MOTIVATION

Being able to motivate yourself can make all the difference between success and failure. This is the quality that will keep you going when things get tough, enabling you to stay on course until you triumphantly cross the finishing line.

FINDING THE WILL

If you can't get started on a task or project, ask yourself whether this is because it's something unappealing but necessary, or whether it's something you want to do but are unsure how to begin.

One or more of the following ideas may help to spur you on to action:

- Tell other people what you're intending to do. Publicizing your plans makes it more difficult to back down or give up.
- Break the job or project down into small, easily achievable steps.
- Make a start on any aspect of the job, without thinking about how long it might take or whether you know how to complete it.
- Think of a dull job that you completed in the past. How did you get going? Did you come to find any aspect of the job satisfying? Can you apply the same strategies to the task you're facing now?

KEEP YOUR EYES ON THE PRIZE

Even if you're highly motivated at the start of a project, enthusiasm can flag if you run into difficulties or a task is proving more complex or taking longer than you imagined.

To help maintain your motivation, keep the end result vividly in mind. If you're working with others, keep talking over how good things will be when you reach completion. If boredom has set in, look for a fresh approach or embark on a new aspect of the project to pique your interest. Draw up a list of tasks, including the ones that have already been accomplished – ticking off items is always a boost to flagging willpower. Finally, celebrate every success with some sort of reward.

THE ATTRACTION OF REWARDS

Much of our behaviour is motivated by the expectation of reward, but this can take many forms, from the direct gratification of payment to the satisfaction of a job well done.

Although "extrinsic" rewards – getting things back from other people – can often be a real encouragement, especially when you're in the middle of a long job, in some cases they can actually reduce motivation. For example, people may pursue material rewards (such as money), only to find themselves demotivated when such rewards fail to fulfil their expectations (see page 97).

"Intrinsic" rewards, which come from achieving goals for their own sake, are ultimately more powerful motivators. Look for aspects of your task that you find especially satisfying – things that you might do simply out of interest or pleasure.

MANAGING TIME

We all have 168 hours available to us each week, yet so often we feel an increasing pressure to fit ever more activities into that limited time. Efficient time management is a vital key to getting things done and avoiding that panicky sense of "too much to do – too little time".

WHERE DID THE TIME GO?

The following principle was originally designed to help people clear the piles of paper from their in-trays or e-mails from their in-boxes – but it's useful for any activity. Apply the 3D rule:

Do it,
Drop it, or
Delegate it.

DELEGATION

Most of us are reluctant to delegate, but letting others take on some of your tasks can help you make better use of your own time. At home, for example, it's easy for family members to stick with the chores they've always done (or not done). Reassess regularly who does what: just because Dan couldn't reach the washing-machine buttons when he was five doesn't mean he can't use the machine when he's fifteen!

Delegation at work can be trickier, but a good delegator will reap the rewards. Assess what you actually spend most of your time doing, and consider whether the jobs that are most mundane for you could be given to less experienced colleagues. Delegation takes planning. You need to allow enough time to teach the other person to perform the task, so it's not something that should be left till the last minute.

DEADLINES

Deadlines concentrate our minds, get us moving and keep us focused. However, if we're under too much time pressure, the increase in stress and anxiety can be counterproductive (as shown in the graph on page 104) and our performance can deteriorate, or we can even freeze in our tracks and stop working altogether.

Look upon a deadline as a positive end to aim at, not a looming monster. Just as you were taught when taking examinations at school, plan your time. Break the task down into chunks, consider the order in which things need to be done (see pages 122–4) and allocate enough time for each element of a task.

If, for some reason, you miss a few key stages or get behind schedule, note down why this has happened and make an immediate choice: either to catch up by a certain date or to devise a completely new schedule – and embark on it with a sense of fresh beginnings.

GO THE EXTRA MILE
The most effective time to work on something is when you've finished it early and have time to go back and improve it, rather than squeezing it in just before the deadline. Typically, if you can leave enough time to give your work a final polish, you'll have the chance to aim for excellence.

THE THIEVES OF TIME

It can be all too easy for other people to deflect you from your course of action by requiring you to respond to their activities and demands. Here are two common ways in which people can steal time from you without even necessarily realizing that they're doing it:

- **Making inappropriate requests** To avoid being swamped by other people's requests, be selective about the ones that you act on. Practise giving a polite but firm "no" to those that are unreasonable, are a lower priority than what you're already doing, or for which you're not the best qualified or most available person.
- **Keeping you waiting** Apply the 15-minute rule: if someone has kept you waiting for more than a quarter of an hour with no explanation, then leave. (Obviously, this is not a hard-and-fast rule, and depends on the person and the situation.) If possible, avoid meeting people on the hour; people are more likely to be late than if you arrange to meet at, say, 10 minutes past the hour. While you're waiting, use the time productively to make calls, send text messages, read or make notes.

TIME YOURSELF

Try wearing a stopwatch for one working day. Each time you start productive work, start the stopwatch, and every time you stop – even for a drink, a chat or a gaze out of the window – stop the timer. At the end of the day you may be surprised at how few productive hours you've really worked despite feeling that you've been hard at work all day.

WATCHING THE CLOCK

Offices are notorious as places where time is badly managed. While a friendly atmosphere is to be valued and "water-cooler chats" can prove fruitful, take stock of just how much time is taken up with distractions, then try some of these tips.

* * * * *

If a meeting's agenda is short (and always ensure the meeting has an agenda), suggest that everyone remain standing.

* * *

Not all meetings are necessary. Suggest, when applicable, a more time-efficient way to discuss a particular issue, such as a telephone or internet conference.

* * *

Try positioning your desk to make it harder for colleagues to gain eye contact as they walk past.

* * *

Keep e-mails short, focused and clear, and avoid ambiguous humour (people may take it the wrong way). File your e-mails according to subject in order to save time relocating them.

* * *

Stand up when talking on the phone. This not only makes you sound more confident, but makes long, lazy chats less likely.

SCHEDULING TASKS

Most challenges involve more than one single act. Almost always there are sub-tasks to be taken into consideration along the way. Approaching these tasks in an organized way is an important factor in successfully achieving your goal.

A PLAN OF ATTACK

Whether you're planning a global takeover or a three-course meal, you'll need to work out a sequence that will enable you to complete all the elements of your project in the right order. A good place to start is to ask yourself the following four questions:

- Which tasks are going to take the longest, and will need to be started earliest?
- Which tasks will I need to have completed before other tasks can be started?
- Which tasks can be conducted in parallel?
- What would be the earliest time that each task could be completed, the expected time, and the latest time?

DRAWING A VARIABLE TIMELINE

With these four questions in mind, you can sketch out a "variable timeline" for your project. This plan will help you to make the best use of your time, and allow for any "worst-case scenarios".

Mark the number of weeks or months from beginning to end of your project. Underneath, draw a block to represent the time for each

Timeline in months

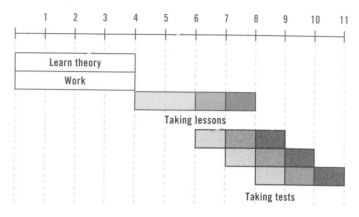

Earliest completion date (if lessons and test go as quickly as possible)
Expected completion date (if lessons and test proceed as expected)
Latest completion date (most pessimistic scenario)

task. If appropriate, break these blocks down further into "earliest time for completion", "expected time", and "latest time".

The simple example shown above is for someone aiming to learn to drive before her next birthday. First, she has to earn the money to pay for lessons (which will take four months), so this task must come before the lessons themselves. However, earning the money can run in parallel with learning and revising her driving theory. She estimates that once she has begun her lessons, she could complete them in as little as two months, or more feasibly in three, but they could take as long as four months. If she then doesn't pass her test the first time, she could retake it at monthly intervals, with three attempts being the worst she anticipates. The timeline thus gives a clear picture of the order of tasks and how long the entire process could take.

Tips on organizing tasks

- If any of your sub-tasks involve creative thinking, schedule them as early as possible and allow plenty of time, to give yourself enough mental space to gestate new ideas (see Chapter 2).
- For sub-tasks that need input from other people, build in plenty of time for each person to do the job and liaise with you, so that any problems or delays won't have adverse effects on your schedule.
- Check whether any tasks or periods of activity fall at an awkward time (such as re-roofing the house in the middle of winter).
- Make adjustments where heavy periods of work cluster together, or when there seem to be periods where no progress is scheduled.
- Build in time to gather information or sharpen skills. Remember this story, about two men competing to see who could chop the most wood in one morning: it wasn't the strongest man who won, but the man who took regular breaks to sharpen his axe.

PERT
The timeline described on the previous pages is based on a method called PERT (program evaluation and review technique), which was developed by the US Navy in the 1950s as part of the project-planning for the Polaris submarine programme. While your goal might not be quite as complex as developing a nuclear submarine, the basic concept still holds good.

FEELINGS AND ACTIONS

A common misconception is to think you have to "feel right" before you can start a task. Thinking like this can cause you to waste a great deal of time and effort in trying to summon up a specific feeling or waiting for it to arrive.

ACTING "AS IF …"

How you feel can certainly affect how you act, but the reverse is also true: your behaviour can drive your feelings, too. If, for example, your mood is a little low, sit up straight, lift your chin up and form a big smile on your face, and you'll actually start to feel happier. The behaviour prompts the change in mood. This technique – acting "as if …" – can fool your subconscious into believing that you really are the way you're pretending to be.

So, rather than waiting until you feel brave enough to embark on something that you want or need to do but fear doing, such as public speaking, asking someone on a date or confronting a noisy neighbour, act as if you're not scared and you'll feel yourself growing in courage.

The same approach can be applied in any situation where you might be waiting for an emotion (happiness, self-confidence, enthusiasm) to arise before you take action. Act like the sort of person who has the qualities you want, and those qualities will appear.

While it's not possible, or necessarily desirable, to exert total control over your feelings, you'll find some useful techniques in Chapter 5 for influencing them, so that they're no longer a barrier.

TEN TIPS TO BEAT PROCRASTiNATION

Procrastination is a common problem, and the more you fall into the habit, the easier it becomes. If you're always putting off doing things you know you must attend to, try these tactics for beating the problem.

1   Let go of perfectionism If you're putting off starting a job because you want to get it perfect, set aside this goal and forge ahead as if your aim is to do it imperfectly. You can always improve it later.

2   Visualize the outcome Picture the benefits of completing your task. Imagine how good you'll feel once it's done.

3   Just do it for 10 minutes It's usually far easier to start something you know will only go on for 10 minutes. Then, once you've started it, you'll tend to work on for longer.

4   Turn off the TV and internet These are two of the greatest time-wasters. Unplug them until you've finished your task.

5   Constant reminders Set a timer to go off, say, every hour, as you're working, so you can stay aware of how fast time is passing.

6   Make it fun Do the most fun (or least painful) part of the task first. This will get you into the swing of it.

7   Catch yourself procrastinating Watch for the moment when you first put off a task. If you can resist that first impulse to delay, it's far easier than trying to fight it later. Resisting procrastination can also become a habit.

8   Do you secretly like procrastinating? Are you addicted to the adrenaline rush of completing a task just in time? If you are, try giving yourself just a little bit more time by creating your own deadline, which is earlier than the real one, so that you have a margin of safety. Get into the habit of starting a project as early as you can, rather than as late as you dare.

9   Accept mistakes as inevitable Fear of making a mistake can deter you from making a start on a new task. Remind yourself that mistakes are a natural, unavoidable part of life that could ultimately teach you how to do something better.

10 Should you really be doing this task? Sometimes procrastination can be a subconscious sign that you want to avoid the activity altogether (beyond sheer laziness). Re-assess whether you really want or need to perform the task.

"Dost thou love life? Then do not squander time, for that's the stuff life is made of."

Benjamin Franklin (1706 90)

THE 80:20 LAW

In many areas of life, 80 per cent of the results flow from just 20 per cent of the actions. This idea is fairly counter-intuitive to most of us: while we might suspect that our lives might need fine-tuning, we rarely expect the difference between vital and non-useful elements to be so large.

WHAT DOES THE LAW MEAN?

While many areas of life don't conform exactly to the 80:20 law – sometimes it's more like 90:10 or 70:30 – the proportions are always more unequal than we'd guess. We mostly wear (approximately) 20 per cent of the clothes we have, listen to 20 per cent of the music tracks we own, spend time with 20 per cent of the people we know, and a tiny minority of websites get the majority of traffic.

The law extends to any area of life in which we seek value, be it the companionship of friends or our earnings over a lifetime. This value clusters together in space and time, which means that it tends mainly to accrue from a minority of possible sources. For example, high-achieving people tend to have a relatively short period in their career in which they produce most of their best work, and a company's profits usually come from a small percentage of its work.

In business, identifying the 20 per cent of products, services or activities that generate 80 per cent of the profits can make a firm more effective. And fixing the 20 per cent of faults that cause 80 per cent of problems can rapidly improve working conditions.

HOW TO HARNESS THE LAW

You can apply the same principles in everyday life. Work smarter, not harder: don't do more overall, but concentrate on the few activities that yield the most rewards. In the midst of everyday distractions, or at times when your schedule gets crowded, keep your mind on the essential 20 per cent to make sure that your plans stay on track.

Try the following suggestions:
- List all your successful actions over the past few months or years. You should find that around 80 per cent of them involved a small area of your life, or resulted from the same few measures. You can then focus your efforts on these highly productive activities.
- If you're working to acquire a new skill, such as speaking a foreign language, concentrating on the 20 per cent of essential elements (such as everyday phrases) will help you to progress faster.
- Over the course of one day, log every single thing you do, and note how much time it takes. Give each action a productivity rating, from 1 (waste of time) to 7 (vital). Use this rating to prioritize the top 20 per cent of tasks and weed out the bottom 20 per cent.

VILFREDO PARETO

The 80:20 law is also known as Pareto's principle, after the 19th-century Italian economist Vilfredo Pareto. He discovered that in society, 80 per cent of property was owned by 20 per cent of the working population. Pareto then found the same pattern of property distribution in each country he studied, in any period of history that he selected.

CONTINUOUS MONITORING

The surest route to success with any goal is to pay close attention to keeping yourself on track. By regularly assessing the effects of past actions, and the likely outcome of future ones, you can make continuous progress and minimize the risk of wasting your energy by going down blind alleys.

LEARNING FROM FEEDBACK

Feedback is the process by which the effect of an action passes back to the person or system that performed the action, causing them to modify their behaviour. Positive feedback will usually encourage them to do more of what works; negative feedback will cause them to curb or stop an unhelpful activity.

Accurate feedback can improve performance. This is how evolution works; this is how brains work; and this is how capitalist economies work, or at least are supposed to. It can work for you too. Feedback gives you clear results, which you can then use as a basis for rational decisions, and prevents you from being deceived by your own biases.

One technique used in product development is the customer survey, in which a firm questions customers for a new product to find out what they like or dislike about that product. You can use similar strategies. When your family has enjoyed a meal that you made, ask what they particularly liked about it. If your job application is rejected, ask for feedback so you can do better on your next one. Test your ideas as often and in as many ways as possible, to gain plenty of feedback.

THE TIME TRAVEL TECHNIQUE

Imagine you could send a message to your former self, a month, a year or five years in the past, concerning a specific course of action that you followed. What advice would you give your former self?

This imaginary feedback can help you to figure out which of your plans worked and which didn't. It can also help you to evaluate decisions, such as whether that college course was worth taking, or whether it was a good idea to have started that relationship. As long as you allow enough time for the results to become clear, you can use the technique for periods of anything from a few minutes to a lifetime.

CHARTING THE FUTURE

You can also use feedback to help yourself chart a course for the future, by means of a technique known as feedback analysis. For every key action or decision, write down what you anticipate might stem from that move. Several months, or a year, down the line, compare expectation and actual result. This analysis can yield illuminating answers that you can then apply to future actions and decisions.

MEDIEVAL FEEDBACK

In 1536 two separate religious movements were founded which together came to dominate Europe: the Calvinist church in the north and the Jesuit order in the south. When business writer Peter Drucker was studying this period of history he discovered what he believes to be the key to their success: feedback analysis. Members of both movements used this technique, and both organizations rapidly flourished.

THE ACTION DAY TECHNIQUE

All too often, life can become an almost robotic cycle of tackling urgent but not necessarily important tasks. If you want to boost your effectiveness, you'll need to try some new tactics. One way to jump-start your mind and body is by having an "action day", in which you work at full throttle.

BREAKING THE BONDS OF FAMILIARITY

Our bodies have an automatic system, called homeostasis, which keeps physical factors such as temperature and fluid levels within safe limits. Our subconscious appears to have a similar mechanism, designed to keep us within familiar patterns of behaviour.

Breaking out of these inbuilt restraints can be hard. Sometimes what we need is not another decision-making or time-management technique but sheer old-fashioned willpower.

ENGAGING YOUR WILLPOWER: THE ACTION DAY

In order to strengthen our willpower, we must develop enough self-control to work toward challenging or long-term goals, rather than pursue momentary pleasures.

One method of generating momentum is the "action day" process invented by self-improvement writer Stuart Goldsmith. An action day can turbo-charge your energy levels as you work toward a goal. Any techniques like this one, that can get you to take action and blast through "to-do" lists, are great for strengthening your willpower.

PLANNING AN ACTION DAY

You first need to prepare for an action day by writing a list of tasks you'd like to complete. Ideally, you should have about 50. The key thing is to choose a wide variety of tasks – small and large, physical and mental, administrative and creative. Write down every last thing you intend to do, from "start composing symphony" to "pay phone bill"!

Organize your action day as follows.

- Start the day at 8am and work through your list until you've completed every item on it – even if this takes you until midnight.
- Remove all temptations from your environment, and prevent disturbance from the telephone, e-mail or any other source.
- No interruptions, distractions or breaks are allowed. No stopping for an hour for lunch: arrange to have something you can eat while you're performing one of your tasks.

An action day is hard work, but take care to stay calm and focused, so you don't feel stressed or panicked. What you can achieve through concentrated action may amaze you!

THE LAW OF INCREASING ENTROPY
In science, the word "entropy" is used to describe a lack of order. Unless energy is put into a system, it will tend to increase in entropy; in other words, the order will disintegrate, like an ice cube melting. Similarly, in life we constantly have to put energy into the things we value in order to keep them functioning properly. An action day can help you to do this.

THE SECRET POWER OF HABITS

Habits are like the servants of your mind: make something into a habit and you free up your conscious mind from having to deal with it. Good habits can turn a task into an automated process that takes less energy to execute.

*   *   *   *   *

Make a list of small but positive activities that would pay big dividends over time. Examples range from being on time for meetings to filing your utility bills as soon as you've paid them. Performed regularly, such activities can noticeably increase your overall effectiveness.

*   *   *

Make a decision to perform one or more of the activities on your list regularly over the course of three months. This should be enough time for it to become a habit.

*   *   *

To help form and reinforce the habit, perform it at a certain place and time each day (or however often you need to do the action).

"The chains of habit are too light to be felt until they are too strong to be broken."

Anonymous

YOUR NEW DECISIVE SELF

Now you've reached the end of the book, you have a range of simple tools that can quickly help you to become more decisive and effective. These tools are self-enhancing: the more you practise them, the stronger they'll grow.

THE BENEFITS OF BEING DECISIVE

It may still take you some time to get used to your new self, even after you've begun to see the benefits of your actions. If you feel your energy or willpower flagging at any point, remember:

- Being decisive gives you greater confidence in yourself, leading to higher self-esteem, and gives others greater confidence in you.
- Becoming decisive is like exercising a muscle – the more you work on it, the "fitter" and more effective you become.
- Being decisive will save you time. Most of the small decisions in life can be taken fairly quickly, and don't actually benefit from lengthy deliberations.

There's a joke that runs: "If you want something done, ask a busy person." As you gain confidence in your ability to make good, quick decisions, you'll get more done; and the more you get done, the more you find you *can* get done. The more time you spend taking action, rather than deliberating or worrying over what to do, the more energetic you'll feel: you'll create a virtuous circle of decisive power. Once that happens, the sky's the limit!

INDEX

FURTHER READING

Writing a book on clear-thinking techniques inevitably builds upon the work of countless thinkers, especially those psychologists pioneering new research on decision-making (most of what we know about the brain has only been discovered in the last two decades). Equally, we have relied on the work of many self-improvement authors for ideas on transforming accurate thinking into effective action. A good starting point for delving further into this work would be to check out some of the titles listed below.

Branden, Nathaniel *The Six Pillars of Self Esteem*, Random House, 2004
Claxton, Guy *Hare Brain, Tortoise Mind*, Fourth Estate, 1998
Eysenck, Hans and Wilson, Glenn *Know Your Own Personality*, Penguin Books, 1991
Gladwell, Malcolm *Blink*, Penguin Books, 2006
Goldsmith, Stuart *Seven Secrets of Millionaires*, Medina Publishing, 2001
Koch, Richard *The Power Laws*, Nicholas Brealey Publishing, 2000
Schwartz, Barry *The Paradox of Choice*, HarperCollins, 2005
Wenger, Win *The Einstein Factor*, Prima Publishing, 1996

AUTHOR'S WEBSITES

For more information on the authors, please visit: www.DarrenBridger.net and www.DrDavidLewis.co.uk

AUTHORS' ACKNOWLEDGMENTS

Many thanks to our colleagues at The Mind Lab, in particular Dan Jones, Steven Matthews, and Hanne Peasgood. Thanks also to Roger, Lynda and Lucy Bridger, Graeme McKeown, Megan, Soffie and Kyrie. We'd like to extend our gratitude to Katie John and Bob Saxton for their superb work in getting the book into its finished form, and to Clare Thorpe for the stylish design. Finally, we are especially grateful to our superbly smart editor, Caroline Ball, for the often mind-stretching task of not only editing but checking the logic of many parts of the book!